Map from Goode's World Atlas
© 1995 by Rand McNally, R. L. 95-S-245

Map from Goode's World Atlas
© 1995 by Rand McNally, R. L. 95-S-245

Enchantment of the World

NEPAL

By Ann Heinrichs

Consultant for Nepal: Leo E. Rose, Ph.D., Professor Emeritus, Political Science, University of California, Oakland; Editor, *Asian Survey*

CHILDREN'S PRESS®
A Division of Grolier Publishing
New York • London • Hong Kong • Sydney
Danbury, Connecticut

Project Editor: Mary Reidy
Design: Jean Blashfield Black
Photo Research: Feldman & Associates, Inc.

Library of Congress Cataloging-in-Publication Data

Heinrichs, Ann
    Nepal / Ann Heinrichs.
       p. cm. — (Enchantment of the world)
    Includes index.
    Summary: Describes the geography, history, culture,
economy, and people of the Asian mountain kingdom of
Nepal.
    ISBN 0-516-02642-0
    1. Nepal—Juvenile literature. [1. Nepal.] I. Title. II.
Series.
DS493.4.H45   1996
954.96—dc20   95-40356
                                    CIP
                                      AC

Picture Acknowledgments:
H.Armstrong Roberts —© Huber, Cover; © V. Clevenger,
9, 10; © Warren Morgan, 18 (top right), 49, 64; © George
Hunter, 40 (left); © Charles May, 82 (left), 93 (right);
© Geopress, 98 (bottom left); © G. Roessler, 80 (bottom),
84 (center)
Tony Stone Images — © Colin Prior, 4, 5 (spread), 31, 101;
© David Austen, 28 (bottom left), 53 (bottom left); © John
Beatty, 32 (top left), 84 (bottom left); © David Sutherland,
38 (left); © Steve Climpson, 40 (right); © Jane Lewis, 76;
© Allan Bramley, 87; © Margaret Gowan, 90; © Osmond, 99

Cameramann International, Ltd. — 6, 28 (top left), 35, 48
(left), 48 (right), 50 (left), 61 (left) 71, (top), 71 (inset),
88 (right), 97 (top), 98 (top left)
Valan Photos — © B. Templeman, 8, 21, 103 (right), 109
(right); © Dr. A Farquhar, 14; © Aubrey Lang, 22 (top right),
22 (top left); © Robert C. Simpson, 23 (center); © Christine
Osborne, 38 (right); © Fred Bruemmer, 84 (top left), 105
(right); © Y.T. Tymstra, 93 (left)
Ira Spring — © Kirkendall/Spring, 12, 24 (right), 47 (left),
53 (top left), 82 (right), 86 (right), 92 (right)
SuperStock International, Inc. — © Steve Vidler, 13, 67, 84
(bottom right); © H.Claude Shostal, 16 (top); © David A.
Northcott, 22 (bottom left); © John Warden, 26;
© Schuster, 36; © Ray Manley, 63; © Chigmaroff/Davison,
86 (left); © Ping Amranand, 97 (inset)
Wide World Photos — 16 (bottom right); 16 (bottom left); 72
(top), 72 (bottom), 75 (left), 79, 89
Root Resources — © Jane P. Downton, 18 (top left); © Byron
Crader, 20 ; © Kenneth W. Fink, 22 (bottom right), 23 (right),
23 (left); © Irene E. Hubbell, 55, 109 (left)
Bettmann Newsphotos — 25, 70 (left), 75 (right), 98 (top
right)
Odyssey — © Robert Frerck, 27, 59, 84 (top right); © Barry
Durand, 61 (right)
Tom Stack & Associates — © Spencer Swanger, 100 (left),
105 (left)
Alison Wright Photography — © Alison Wright, 24 (left), 28
(middle left), 30, 32 (top right), 33, 34, 39, 42, 45 (left), 45
(right), 47 (right), 51, 56, 78, 80 (top), 92 (left), 100 (right),
102, 103 (left), 106 (right)
Words and Pictures — © Carl Purcell, 28 (middle right), 28
(top right), 50 (right), 53 (right), 88 (left), 111
North Wind Picture Archives — 68
UPI/Bettmann—70 (right)
Viewpoints, Inc. — © Porterfield/Chickering, 94, 98 (bottom right), 106 (left)

Cover: A Sherpa woman and her yak

The snow-covered peaks of the Everest region in Nepal's Sagarmatha National Park

TABLE OF CONTENTS

Swayambhunath stupa, or shrine, near Kathmandu stands on the Swayambhu hill, which has been regarded as sacred for 2,000 years.

Chapter 1

ABODE OF THE SNOW

According to legend, there was once a mountainous land called *Himarant* or *Himalaya*, meaning "Abode of the Snow." It lay between the great Himalayas and the lesser Mahabharat range to the south.

The *Swayambhunath Purana*, an ancient Nepalese chronicle, tells of a lake that once covered this land. In the Golden Age, long before our present time, the first Buddha threw a lotus seed into the lake. Eighty thousand years later, an earthquake shook the land. An island rose up from the center of the lake, and upon it was the lotus, now blossomed into a great, thousand-petaled blue flower. Within the lotus was a dazzling flame, the Swayambhu—the eternal, primordial, self-existent, self-created one—radiating a warm and brilliant light.

Along came Manjushri, a *bodhisattva*, or living embodiment of the Buddha—to worship at the holy site. So that pilgrims could more easily reach the spot, Manjushri cut a gorge through the mountains to drain the lake. The water rushed out through the gorge, revealing a lush, fertile valley where the lake's bed had been. This is the Kathmandu Valley. The gorge is Chobar Gorge, and the rushing waters pouring through it form the Bagmati River on its southward course from the Kathmandu Valley into India.

Swayambhunath stupa (a Buddhist shrine), on a hill just west

A lotus flower painted on a rock and a prayer flag stuck into the ground greet travelers along the Dudi Kush River. Nepal is a very religion-centered nation.

of Kathmandu, stands on the spot where the legendary lotus once grew. Two different stories tell how this came to be. In one, the lotus became Swayambhunath hill and the light became the stupa. In the other, a holy monk foresaw the dark and sinful age that was to come. He placed a stone over the flame and built the stupa on the stone. Either way, Swayambhunath is one of the holiest shrines in Nepal.

Tibetan Buddhist literature speaks of *beyuls,* or hidden valleys, nestled within the Himalayas. Protected from worldly strife, the beyul is a luxurious paradise of comforts, riches, and harmony. Some beyuls are said to be located in northeastern Nepal's Khumbu region. Only those who follow mysterious directions and a rigorous spiritual path are able to find them.

Swathed in myth since its earliest times, Nepal remained something of a mystery to the outside world until the middle of the twentieth century. Its own rulers, themselves enchanted with their tiny kingdom, jealously guarded it against colonization.

Nepal's official name is the Kingdom of Nepal—*Sri Nepala Sarkar,* or *Nepal Adhirajya* in Nepali. One of the world's poorest nations in economic terms, Nepal is one of the richest in spirituality and natural splendors. It is said that there are more shrines and temples in Nepal than there are homes, more festivals than there are days in a year. On a clear day in the tropical southern plains, one can see the shrouded, icy peaks of the massive Himalayas at Nepal's northernmost extremes. Side by side within these borders, people of countless ancient cultures find a home in the "Abode of the Snow."

Basket sellers at the mountain village of Namche Bazar in the "Abode of the Snow"

Chapter 2

STEAMY JUNGLES, MYSTICAL PEAKS

Nepal is a rugged, mountainous country in southern Asia, with most of its territory lying on the southern slopes of the Himalaya mountains. It is completely surrounded by land. To the east, south, and west is India, and to the northeast is Sikkim. Along most of the northern border lies Tibet (officially, the Tibetan Autonomous Region of the People's Republic of China). Nepal is long and thin, measuring about 500 miles (805 kilometers) from west to east and 150 miles (241 kilometers) from north to south. With an area of 56,827 square miles (147,182 square kilometers), it is about the same size as the state of Arkansas.

GEOGRAPHIC REGIONS

Nepal has three major geographic regions, all spreading across the country from west to east. The elevation rises dramatically from the southern plains to the northern mountain peaks. Nowhere else on earth are there such extreme differences in altitude.

Opposite page: Wild poinsettias seen against a mountainside that has been meticulously terraced to gain all the farmland possible

Royal Chitwan National Park in the Terai offers visitors tropical jungle, within sight of the highest mountains in the world.

The narrow strip of low, fertile plains across southern Nepal is the Terai region. This is the northernmost part of the Ganges Basin plain. Waters in the Terai's rivers and streams eventually flow into India's Ganges River and, finally, into the Bay of Bengal.

Most of Nepal's farm products are grown in the lush fields of the southern Terai. *Terai,* or *Tarai,* means "damp" or "fever." Steamy tropical jungles cover much of this region. Nepal's lowest point, in the eastern Terai, is 230 feet (70 meters) above sea level.

In the northern Terai, marshes and forests take over as the land slopes upward toward the hills of the Siwalik Range (also called the Churia Hills).

The central strip of land running through Nepal is hill country. Here rise the Mahabharat and Siwalik mountain ranges and the rocky foothills and lower ranges of the high Himalayas. Swift mountain streams course through gorges in the mountains. There are many broad, high valleys nestled throughout the hill region. One is the Kathmandu Valley. Here, in east-central Nepal, is the capital city of Kathmandu. In west-central Nepal, the Pokhara Valley lies in the shadow of the Annapurna Range. There are four main peaks in that range, numbered I through IV.

The Kathmandu Valley is the most heavily populated region of Nepal.

Across all of northern Nepal are the Himalayas themselves, their jagged crests outlining Nepal's border with Tibet. The high mountain valleys at the country's northern reaches are an extension of the arid Tibetan Plateau.

THE HIMALAYAS

To both Hindus and Buddhists, the Himalayas are sacred. They believe that some of their most powerful deities dwell

Annapurna, as seen from a farmyard near Pokhara

among the Himalayan peaks, which they call the "Abode of the Gods." Gaurisangkar is the home of the Hindu god Shiva and his consort, Parvati. Annapurna, the goddess of plenty, lives atop Annapurna I, while the elephant-headed Ganesh, son of Shiva, resides on Ganesh Himal I. Many Himalayan peaks remain off-limits to climbers even today, lest the resident gods retaliate with mountain slides, floods, or disease. People who climb Mount Everest are advised to make offerings to the goddess Sagarmatha as they make their way up to her home.

The full Himalaya Range stretches some 1,550 miles (2,500 kilometers), from the Indian state of Jammu and Kashmir in the west, to Burma in the east. Its highest points are in Nepal, where eight of the world's ten tallest peaks rise. Crowning them all is Mount Everest. At 29,028 feet (8,848 meters) above sea level, Everest is the highest mountain in the world.

Mountaineers have a special awe and respect for "eight thousanders"—mountains more than 8,000 meters (26,247 feet) high. From west to east, Nepal's "eight-thousanders" are Dhaulagiri I (26,810 feet; 8,172 meters), Annapurna I (26,504 feet; 8,078 meters), Manaslu I (26,760 feet; 8,156 meters), Cho Oyu (26,750 feet; 8,153 meters), Everest (29,028 feet; 8,848 meters), Lhotse I (27,923 feet; 8,511 meters), Makalu I (27,824 feet; 8,481 meters), and Kanchenjunga I (28,208 feet; 8,598 meters).

MOUNT EVEREST

Mount Everest's peak marks the Nepal-Tibet border. The Nepalese call it *Sagarmatha,* meaning "Mother of the Universe." Similarly, Tibetans call it *Chomolunga,* or "Mother Goddess of the World." In 1852 British surveyors established that Everest's peak was the highest point on earth. They named it after Sir George Everest, the surveyor-general of India who had directed the mountain survey.

Before Nepal opened its borders to outsiders in 1950, climbers could approach Mount Everest only from its north side in Tibet. The first Everest expeditions were organized in the 1920s and 1930s. The climbers hired Sherpas in India, then traveled from eastern India northward into Tibet. Then they hiked west to Everest to climb its northern face.

"BECAUSE IT IS THERE"

In 1921 British mountaineer Sir George Mallory launched the first expedition to conquer the peak. Asked why he would want to take on such a grueling challenge, Mallory replied with his now-legendary quip: "Because it is there."

In 1953 Edmund Hillary (left) became the first person to climb the peak of Mount Everest. In the photo below, he is seen at the left with Tenzing Norgay, his Sherpa guide, at the right, showing the man in the middle the route they followed up the mountain.

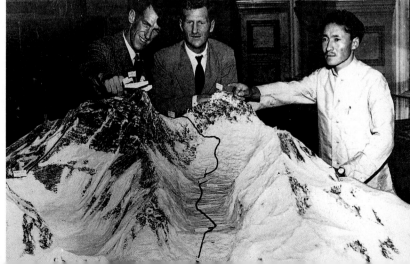

The task would not be easy. Its summit swathed in clouds, Everest appeared just one among hundreds of craggy peaks. As Mallory observed, "It would be necessary in the first place to find the mountain."

Mallory and his climbing partner, Andrew Irvine, did find it. On June 8, 1924, the two left their high base camp to go for the summit. They disappeared into the clouds and were never seen again.

Over the next three decades many more attempts were made to conquer Everest's peak. Many climbers fell victim to frostbite or to oxygen shortage in the high, thin air. Some fell to their deaths. It was not until 1953 that Edmund Hillary and his Sherpa guide, Tenzing Norgay, at last reached the summit. A New Zealand beekeeper and avid mountain-climber, Hillary had practiced for years—in New Zealand, in the Alps, and on other Himalayan peaks. As soon as Hillary got back to Kathmandu, he was greeted with news that Queen Elizabeth II of Great Britain would bestow on him the honor of knighthood for his feat.

Many have attempted the climb since then. Climbers come from Great Britain, Japan, Austria, France, Poland, Germany, and Italy, as well as from India, China, and Nepal. Many have failed, but a few have succeeded. Some landmark successes: In 1965 Nawang Gopmbu, a Sherpa of India, was the first to reach the summit twice. In 1975 Junko Tabei of Japan was the first woman to scale the peak. In 1980 Reinhold Messner of Italy made the first solo climb. A record was set on May 12, 1992, when twenty-eight climbers from five different expeditions reached the summit on a single day! More try the climb every year. Why do they do it? Maybe just "because it is there."

The distant Bagmati River (above) becomes a friendly river used in religious ceremonies when it reaches Kathmandu. The Karnali River of western Nepal (right) can usually be crossed only by rough suspension bridges.

RIVER SYSTEMS

Nepal's major rivers run generally from north to south. Most have their sources not in the Himalayas but in the high Tibetan Plateau to the north. Melting ice in the mountains swells them, and they eventually empty into India's Ganges River and finally into the Bay of Bengal. Traders have followed these rivers since ancient times, and settlers have made their villages along them.

Three major river systems drain Nepal. In the east is the Kosi and its seven tributaries. In the center of the country is the Gandak River system. (Its name changes to Narayani in the south.) The Karnali (Gogra) and its tributaries flow through western Nepal.

Different branches or segments of the same river may go by variant names. For instance, streams that feed into the Kosi at various stages of its southward course have the names Dudha Kosi, Sun Kosi, and Sapta Kosi. Similarly, there are the Kali Gandaki, the Krishna Gandaki, and the Budhi Gandaki.

Coursing through Nepal's mountains and hills, these rivers have carved out deep gorges and broad valleys. In the valleys is rich farmland. The Pokhara Valley of central Nepal is one of the country's finest agricultural regions. It is drained by the Seti River. The Valley of Nepal, where Kathmandu is situated, is actually the bed of an ancient lake. Covering about 300 square miles (780 square kilometers), the Valley of Nepal (also called Kathmandu Valley) is another important agricultural region.

Water pollution is a serious problem for rivers in the Terai, in the Kathmandu and Pokhara valleys, and in other regions that are developing quickly. Human and animal wastes make these waters dangerously unfit to drink.

CLIMATE

Nepal is located on the same latitude as the Arabian desert, but within its borders, it has almost every climate in the world, from subtropical to arctic. Both altitude and geographical location determine Nepal's weather.

Both the Terai and the Kathmandu Valley are said to have three seasons—hot, rainy, and cold. Summers in the Terai are subtropical and winters are mild. The swamps, jungles, and forests are hot and very humid. At elevations between 4,000 and 11,000 feet (1,219 and 3,353 meters), the climate is temperate, with the lower areas warmer and the higher regions cooler.

Much of the Kathmandu Valley is in the temperate zone. January temperatures in the capital range from 36 to 64 degrees Fahrenheit (2 to 18 degrees Celsius). Temperatures in July, the hottest month, range from 68 to 84 degrees Fahrenheit (20 to 29

Rice farms in the Kathmandu Valley during the dry season

degrees Celsius). The rainy season in the Kathmandu Valley lasts from June through September. Most of the valley's annual precipitation of 60 inches (152 centimeters a year) falls at this time. The colder winter months follow, until March, when warmer weather moves in. About 100 inches (254 centimeters) of rain fall each year in the Pokhara Valley, as monsoon winds collide with the Annapurna Range.

The high Himalayas, above 16,000 feet (4,877 meters), are covered with snow and ice all year. The air temperature is always below freezing. The high valleys are cold, treeless, and desertlike.

Summer monsoons (strong southerly winds) bring wind and torrential rains to the southern plains, the hills, and the central valleys. This is when Nepal receives 80 percent of its precipitation. During monsoon season, flooding can be a serious problem in low-lying areas. Rivers and streams in the Terai often flood during the monsoon season. The 1993 floods took more than a thousand Nepalese lives and destroyed countless acres of crops. The monsoons blow inland from the Bay of Bengal, off India's eastern

Some Nepalese porters, working high on the snowy peaks, choose to climb barefooted.

coast, through India and into Nepal. Thus, the eastern Terai's monsoons are fiercer than the central valley's. Precipitation there is 70 to 75 inches (178 to 190 centimeters) a year. Western Nepal is much drier than the east, with only about 30 to 35 inches (76 to 89 centimeters) of rainfall a year.

ANIMALS

Nepal's endangered species include the snow leopard, tiger, Asian elephant, pygmy hog, Indian rhinoceros, Assam rabbit, swamp deer, pheasant, and gavial (a kind of crocodile). World Wildlife Fund programs in Nepal are working to protect these and other species and to make sure their habitats continue to provide them with food and shelter.

In the forests of Nepal's Terai region live tigers, leopards, hyenas, jackals, rhesus monkeys, gaur (wild oxen), and deer. The deer species include sambar, chital (or axis) deer, and swamp deer. There are only a few hundred Indian rhinoceroses left in the

The Indian rhinoceros (top left) and the Indian tiger (top right) are both rare sights in the jungle of the Terai. The snow leopard (bottom left) and the Himalayan tahr (bottom right) are animals of the high mountain slopes, often found above the tree line.

world, and about half live in the Terai's Chitwan district. Poachers have long overhunted this species for its horns, which are believed to have medicinal value.

Wildlife in Nepal's central valley is rather sparse because people have cleared and developed so much of this land. In the southeastern section of the valley, however, there is enough wildlife for hunting. In the remaining central forests, there are still

The Himalayan black bear, or moon bear (left), lives in the forests below the tree line, where the griffon vultures (center) fly. The swamp deer, or barasingha (right), is a lowland animal related to the American wapiti.

some black and brown bears, leopards and other cats, and muntjacs, also called barking deer.

The lower slopes of the Himalayas are home to wolves, snow leopards, wild sheep, tahrs (wild goats), ghorals (goat-antelopes), Himalayan chamois, marmots, tailless mouse-hares, and musk deer. Tahrs are protected in Sagarmatha National Park. The musk deer is hunted for its musk pods, located under the male's tail. Musk, used to make medicines, incense, and perfumes, fetches a high price in the marketplace.

Birds at this altitude include pheasants, hill partridges, flower-peckers, sunbirds, and minivets. Golden eagles, lammergeier hawks, and Himalayan griffon vultures also live in the highlands.

Mountain climbers have found small black spiders at altitudes as high as 22,500 feet (6,858 meters). In general, however, almost

The pheasant (above) is the national bird of Nepal. Tame rhesus monkeys (right) are often found on the grounds of temples where they are fed and honored. They are regarded as sacred by the Hindus.

no animal life is found in the highest reaches of the Himalayas—unless the legends of the yeti are true.

YETI—THE ABOMINABLE SNOWMAN

The yeti—also known as the Abominable Snowman—is said to be a huge, apelike or bearlike creature of the craggy Himalayan slopes. Many Sherpas—as well as Western hikers and tribal people in the northwest and in Sikkim—have seen what they believe to be its enormous footprints. A few claim they have actually seen the white hairy beast. One Himalayan monastery had what the monks believed was a yeti's skeleton hand. Others claim to possess yeti scalps.

In 1960 Sir Edmund Hillary set out on an expedition to solve the mystery of the yeti once and for all. He and his team of scientists concluded that any evidence of the yeti's existence was

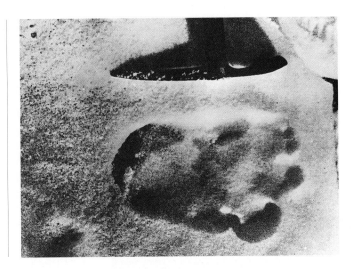

In 1958, climbers on Mount Everest photographed this track, which might have been made by a yeti, or Abominable Snowman. It is about the length of the ax head positioned next to it.

either left by another animal or fabricated as a hoax. Nevertheless, the Sherpas and others still swear that the yeti haunts the high Himalayas.

PLANT LIFE

Nepal's plant life varies with changes in climate and altitude. Forestlands cover almost one-third of the country, and the government owns most of them. Deciduous trees in the subtropical forests of the Terai include khair, sisu, somal, and sal. Lac insects, which feed on sal leaves, deposit a substance used to make shellac and varnishes. Farther north, there are pines, oaks, rhododendrons, and poplars.

The lower slopes of the Himalayas are heavily forested with spruce, fir, cypress, juniper, and birch. By stripping junipers for firewood, campers and hikers have caused a serious soil erosion problem in the Himalayan foothills. Strict conservation laws have slowed the stripping, but it continues to be a serious problem.

The tree line or timberline, at about 16,000 feet (4,877 meters), is the point beyond which trees can no longer survive. Above this point grow mosses and ferns and also wildflowers such as primula, cotoneaster, and white erica.

Much of Nepal's central valley has been stripped of trees and bushes. But beautiful wildflowers remain, including orchids, lilies, poppies, and anemones.

The rhododendron is Nepal's national flower. At lower elevations, the blossoms are bright red; higher up, they become purple and pink. At the highest elevations, they are yellow, cream-colored, and white. Dwarf rhododendrons grow in the higher mountain regions, and on the lower slopes are spectacular tree rhododendrons. These can grow as high as 40 feet (12 meters).

A rhododendron, Nepal's national flower

Chapter 3

THE PEOPLE

In 1994 Nepal's population was estimated at about 21,042,000 people. This makes for an overall average of about 370 people per square mile (143 per square kilometer). There really is no "average" area, though, because the north is lightly populated and the lower hills and the Terai are heavily populated. Only about 10 percent of Nepalese live in cities and towns. Kathmandu, the capital and largest city, had an estimated population of 422,000 people in 1987. Nepal's population is growing at the rate of about 2.4 percent a year.

LANGUAGE

Nepali is the official language of Nepal. It is spoken by about 40 percent of the people as their mother tongue. Nepali is closely related to Hindi, a north Indian language. Like Hindi,

The religious symbols have been carved on this prayer stone found in the northern mountain region.

Some of the faces of Nepal: The woman at top left is an immigrant from nearby India. The Tharu woman at center left is placing coconut strips out to dry. The seller of religious objects at bottom left is a Newar man in Prajapati. Top center: An old man smoking; top right: a city woman carrying wood; bottom right: a Hindu mother and child

Nepali is derived from ancient Sanskrit, the "mother language" of most Indian dialects. Nepali has many "loan words" from Hindi, Newari, and other languages and dialects of the region, as well as from Sanskrit. The Nepali writing system, Devagnagari, is the same as that used for Hindi.

About 30 percent of the people speak various dialects of Hindi or Bengali, and another 30 percent speak Newari or hill tribal languages and various Tibetan-derived languages. At least eighteen other languages spoken in Nepal are listed in the census, and probably another twenty are spoken by small ethnic groups.

ETHNIC GROUPS AND CASTES

Over the centuries, the ancestors of today's Nepalese people arrived in waves of migration from India, Tibet, and Central Asia. Throughout the country, more than thirty-five separate ethnic groups have been identified. The Nepalese generally fall within one of two broad classifications: Indo-Aryan, people from the Indian subcontinent of Asia, and Mongolian, people from northern and eastern Asia.

Newars are the predominant people of the Kathmandu Valley, and Tharus live mainly in the western and west-central Terai. These two peoples were among the first to arrive in what is now Nepal, migrating up from northern India.

Tribal groups of the central hill region include the Gurung, Magar, Rai, Limbu, Yakha, and Sunwar people. From these tribes the British army recruited its famous Gurkha soldiers in the nineteenth century. Military service is still a preferred occupation among these people, but agriculture is their mainstay.

A Gaines man, who belongs to the occupational caste of musicians

The most prominent tribal people of northern Nepal are the Thakalis and the Sherpas. Both groups are of Tibetan origin. Both also look back to a long tradition as traders between Tibet to the north and India to the south. Inhabiting the upper Kali Gandaki River region, the Thakalis make their living today as farmers and yak herders.

Besides the ethnic, or tribal, identities apparent in Nepal, people also may be identified by their rank within the Hindu religion's caste system, a way of classifying people. This becomes very complicated. In some cases, entire tribes belong to a certain caste. In other cases, people who hold certain occupations are regarded as belonging to certain occupational castes.

To further complicate matters, the occupational castes of the central hills and those of the southern Terai plains do not have equal status, even when the occupations are the same. In the hills, for instance, makers of gold and silver ornaments rank very low in the religious and social hierarchy. The same craftsworkers in the plains region, however, rank the highest among all the craftsworker castes. In the Terai, which borders northern India, the caste system is much more complex than in the hills. There are many more occupational castes and subdivisions within castes.

Sherpa women carrying heavily laden baskets for a group of visitors on trek

TIGERS OF THE SNOW

For centuries, Sherpas transported trade goods across the Himalayas, loaded down with backpacks and leading trains of pack animals. Tibet was their Buddhist homeland, and they traded with Hindu India. The Himalayas were simply an obstacle to be dealt with in between. Strong, hardy, and agile, they were nicknamed "Tigers of the Snow."

The Sherpas of northern and eastern Nepal are still the most expert porters in the Himalayan region. They are highly regarded as hardy mountaineers and are valued as porters and guides on mountain-climbing expeditions. Some Sherpas now have organized Everest expeditions of their own. Probably the best-known Sherpa is Tenzing Norgay, whose expedition with Edmund Hillary was the first to reach the top of Mount Everest. Most

Rural Nepalese children leaving their farm for school (left),
and a Nepalese teenage boy at his desk in a city school (right)

Sherpas, however, live as farmers and herders. They may be away
from their homes for as much as six months at a time, returning
before the monsoons begin.

EDUCATION AND LITERACY

Less than half of all Nepalese people—40 percent—can read
and write. But there is a great difference between male and female
literacy rates. About 60 percent of men and boys over age fifteen
can read and write, but only about 20 percent of Nepal's women
and girls are literate.

A United Nations worker giving visual literacy tests to rural women

Nepal, like many other developing countries, is trying to improve the opportunities for girls to get an education. The Nepalese government has set "universal primary education" as a major goal. This means schools that are better, easier to reach, and attended by all. Another goal is to provide free secondary schools.

The government already provides free public schools. By law, children must attend five years of primary (elementary) school, beginning at age six. Then at age eleven they begin five years of secondary school—a two-year segment followed by a three-year segment. However, only about three-fifths of school-age children attend primary school. Even fewer—about one-fourth of the school-age population—go to secondary school. The low attendance is mainly because families need the children to work. There are twice as many boys in Nepalese schools as there are girls.

Nepal's two universities are Tribhuvan University in Kathmandu and the Mahendra Sanskrit University in Beljhundi. Tribhuvan has branches in the Nepal hills and the Terai, but degrees are conferred and examinations conducted only at the Kathmandu Valley

This small child being weighed at an international health post supported by a children's fund may be luckier than many small children in Nepal, where the death rate for young children is about one in every ten.

campus. In 1990, Nepal's total college enrollment was about 103,000 students.

PUBLIC HEALTH

About one of every ten children born in Nepal dies as an infant. It has been estimated that half of Nepalese children die before the age of five. They are victims of poor nutrition, diarrhea and other gastrointestinal disorders, and various other diseases.

Stomach and intestinal problems are the most common medical problems in Nepal. Malaria is a danger to natives and visitors alike, especially in the warm, steamy Terai. However, mosquitoes that carry malaria do not survive well at higher altitudes.

On average, Nepalese men live to the age of fifty-four. Nepalese women's life expectancy is a year or two shorter, partly

In most towns, people go to a central water source to obtain water for bathing, washing clothes, and drinking. They have to carry water supplies back to their homes in large containers.

because the hardships of childbirth take a toll on their overall health. This may seem like a short life span, but health conditions in Nepal have improved tremendously in recent decades. In the 1950s the average life expectancy in Nepal was twenty-eight years! This was mainly due to the high infant mortality rate, which has been greatly reduced since then.

The Nepalese government is trying to encourage its citizens to accept Western medical practices. Unfortunately, there is a severe shortage of doctors and hospitals. In 1990 there was an average of one doctor and four hospital beds for every twenty thousand Nepalese. Those who do accept Western-style treatment usually keep their faith in traditional healers at the same time.

Visitors to Nepal need to get immunization shots or take precautions against dysentery, malaria, typhoid, hepatitis, and rabies. Hikers face their own set of dangers. They may suffer from sore feet and blisters, overexposure to cold, heat exhaustion, or snow blindness.

Chapter 4

RELIGION, CULTURE, AND WAY OF LIFE

Nepal is an obviously religious country. Everywhere, from cities to rural villages, are monasteries, temples, stupas, prayer flags, and other signs of religious devotion. Nepal is the only official Hindu kingdom in the world. This can be misleading, though. About half the population follow both Hindu and Buddhist religious practices and use tribal shamans, Buddhist lamas, and Hindu Brahmans on different occasions and for different reasons. In the past the government has classified these people as Hindus, but that probably will be changed in the next government census.

A small but strong minority—around 10 percent—are Buddhists. Nearly all of Nepal's Buddhists follow the form of Buddhism that is practiced in Tibet. About 5 percent are Muslims or members of Terai or hill-tribe animist religions.

The Nepalese freely accept one another's religious practices. Religious festivals of many different sects are celebrated openly. Anyone is welcome to benefit from them, as a source of inspiration,

Opposite page: This Hindu holy man, or saddhu, is one of many who support their religious lives by accepting donations from passersby.

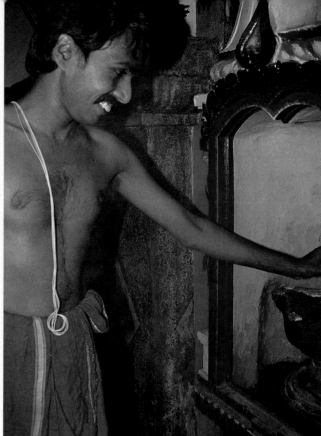

The twelve-armed Black Shiva is an outdoor Hindu shrine in Durbar Square in Kathmandu (left). A young Brahman, or seeker after knowledge (right); Hindu men often start their training in Brahmanism as young boys.

as a matter of interest, or for the sheer enjoyment of the colorful displays.

HINDUISM

The roots of Hinduism in Nepal go back to Aryan people who invaded India from the north in the second millennium B.C. These people recorded their beliefs in the *Vedas*, a collection of more than a thousand sacred hymns. Aryan and local beliefs blended to produce Hinduism. Human society is ranked according to castes, or classes. From highest to lowest, they are the Brahmans (priests), Chhetris or Kshatriyas (warriors), Vaisyas (artisans and traders), and Sudras (serfs). Many variations of the caste system are observed, but their basic plan of ordered classes is the same.

Reincarnation is a central doctrine of Hinduism. By the law of karma, or spiritual cause-and-effect, leading a good and dutiful life earns rebirth at a higher level. Bad living sends a person backward in the cycle. Dharma is the set of ethical rules that apply to one's station in life. Through spiritual growth and compassionate living, a Hindu aims to earn release from the cycle of reincarnation.

The principal deities of Hinduism are Brahma (the creator), Vishnu (the preserver), and Shiva (the destroyer). Hundreds of other gods and goddesses fill out the Hindu pantheon. A single deity also may appear in various forms or manifestations. A god incarnated in human form is an avatar. Hindus make *puja,* or ritual offerings to the gods, often consisting of grains and red powder. These substances are ground to make a paste—*tika*—that is applied to the forehead as a spiritual symbol.

A young Hindu woman applying tika—a red powder paste—to her forehead as puja, an offering to the gods

A Golden Buddha statue dressed by the faithful for a festive occasion (left), and two Buddhist monks, one a child (above), in the mountains

BUDDHISM

Buddhism arose in the sixth century B.C. It is a well-organized religious system based on a philosophy, or way of life, that grew out of Hinduism. Although Buddhists apply the name *Buddha*—meaning "Enlightened One"—to legendary spiritual beings, there was also an actual, historical Buddha.

Prince Siddhartha Gautama was born in Lumbini, in southern

Nepal, in about 543 B.C. His father, a warrior-chief of the Sakya clan, ruled the kingdom of Kapilavastu. The prince spent his early life in absolute luxury, never venturing outside the royal palace and gardens. He married a princess and they had a child. One day, at the age of twenty-nine, he took a ride out into the countryside for the first time. There he encountered an old man, a sick man, and a corpse.

Shaken by the sight of such misery, he left home and wandered through India searching for an answer to the human condition. After five years, enlightenment struck him. The things of life, he realized, are passing illusions. Too much attachment to these illusions causes both pleasure and pain. Now, as the Buddha, or Enlightened One, he began to preach the Middle Way of right living, based on Four Noble Truths and the Eightfold Path. By following these teachings, one could attain *nirvana*—an end to suffering and a release from the cycle of rebirth.

Although Buddhism gradually gave way to Hinduism in India, it remained alive in Nepal. The Mahayana sect of Buddhism is the prevalent form. Mahayanism introduced the idea of the *bodhisattva*, a person who has earned nirvana but chooses to remain in human life to help others in their path to enlightenment.

SHAMANISM

It is hard to say how many Nepalese people follow ancient, ancestral belief systems. Many Nepalese Hindus and Buddhists also cling to ages-old spiritual practices such as ancestor worship, animism (worship of the spirits in nature), or shamanism at the same time.

This shaman is a refugee from Tibet, living in Nepal. He wears a special hat to help him enter the trance state in order to help his client.

Shamanism has been called Nepal's "third religion." Its practice is widespread, especially in small villages and rural areas. The shaman is part psychologist, part fortune-teller, and part doctor. Shamanists believe that by going into a trance and entering the spirit world, the shaman can discover which spirit afflicts his or her client, and why. This points the way to the cure or to the actions to be taken to remedy the problem. A shaman may also choose to be possessed by a certain spirit—perhaps the spirit of an honored member of the community who has died—to understand the past or see the future.

For many Nepalese, the *jhankri*, or shamanistic healer, is the "doctor" of first resort. Going into a trance, the jhankri contacts the evil or mischievous spirit afflicting the patient. The jhankri may threaten the spirit, bargain with it, or just come to understand it.

CALENDARS

Five different calendar systems are used in Nepal. The country's official calendar—-for businesses, government, and national festivals—is the Vikram Samvat. It is broken into twelve months of twenty-nine to thirty-two days each, based on the cycles of the moon. A different Hindu deity is the ruler of each month. One's spiritual outlook waxes and wanes within each month along with the moon. The half-month when the moon is shrinking from full toward new is a time of caution, darkness, and bad fortune. When the moon is growing, prospects are good.

Within each year, and also every nineteen years, adjustments are made to bring the calendar in tune with solar cycles. A government committee is in charge of devising the proper calendar for each coming year.

The starting point for the Vikram Samvat is reckoned from the year 57 B.C., when northern India's legendary King Vikramaditya came to power. His day of victory, celebrated in mid-April, marks the New Year. Because the Vikram Samvat is fifty-seven years ahead of the Western (Gregorian) calendar, the Nepalese celebrated their year 2000 in the Western year 1943. The Vikram Samvat system has a seven-day week, with the days named for the sun, the moon, and five planets.

Nepal's Newar people follow the Nepal Samvat, or Newar Samvat, a calendar with a starting point in A.D. 879 under the Malla kings. It, too, is based on lunar and solar cycles, with October's or November's full moon marking the New Year. A third calendar, Shakya Samvat, dates from A.D. 79, the year the Indian king Salivahan ascended to the throne. Nepal's astrologers use this calendar to reckon their predictions.

Many Nepalese observe the complex Tibetan calendar, called the Kalacakra ("Wheel of Time"). Based on principles of Tantrism, it breaks time into sixty-year cycles. Each year is associated with one of twelve animals. In addition, one of the five elements (earth, water, fire, wood, and iron) is matched with each two successive years—a masculine year and a feminine year. The Tibetan New Year begins, usually, with February's full moon.

Finally, there is the Gregorian calendar, with its New Year's Day fixed at January 1.

FESTIVALS

Most festivals in Nepal are religious celebrations honoring a god or goddess. Whether a given feast is Hindu, Buddhist, or animist, members of all groups freely join in the devotions and festivities. There are seasonal festivals, linked to planting and harvesting times. Other festivals are rooted in myths from ancient folklore. There also are festivals to commemorate important historical events. Because they are figured on a lunar calendar, the exact dates of festivals change from year to year.

A central part of almost every festival is puja. To perform puja, worshipers gather at a shrine and offer prayers, perform religious rituals, and present the deity with such gifts as flowers, incense, red powder, grains and other farm products, and sacrificial animals. Women dress in their finest clothes and jewelry for puja. In some festivals, an image of the god or goddess is carried through the streets in an elaborate chariot. These processions, or *jatra*, may go on for days or even weeks. Temples may serve ritual meals (*bhoj*).

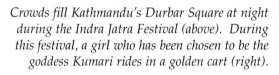

Crowds fill Kathmandu's Durbar Square at night during the Indra Jatra Festival (above). During this festival, a girl who has been chosen to be the goddess Kumari rides in a golden cart (right).

Nepal's biggest celebration is the New Year festival, occurring in April or May. In Bhaktapur, it coincides with the spectacular, days-long Biskit festival. The Newari enshrine images of their gods Bhairava and Bhadrakali in carts so huge that it takes dozens of men to haul them in procession. The climax is a tug-of-war to send a tall pole made from a tree trunk crashing to the ground, bringing luck for the coming year.

Meanwhile, in the nearby village of Thimi, hundreds of people covered with ritual orange powder gather in the early morning for a torchlight procession around the Bal Kumari pagoda. Later the same day a procession of the mother goddesses Mahakala and Mahalakshmi takes place.

In May or June the festival of the Red Machhendranath, patron god of the Kathmandu Valley, is celebrated. The figure of the god, honored for bringing rain to the drought-parched valley, is paraded through the streets of Patan for a month. Around this same time, festivities honoring Buddha's birthday—Buddha

Jayanti—center around Swayambhunath stupa.

August or September brings the eight-day festival of Indra Jatra. Celebrants erect a tall pole before the royal palace and pray to Indra, the god of rain, to spare their crops from destruction by the monsoon. Through the streets a chariot bears the Kumari, a little girl judged to be the reincarnation of the goddess Durga.

Dasain, in September or October, is a fifteen-day national festival celebrating Rama's triumph over evil spirits. (Rama was an avatar of the god Vishnu.) Animals are sacrificed at the shrines of Durga, who aided Rama in his battle. During Tihar (the Festival of Light), in October or November, brothers and sisters honor and pray for each other. Thousands of lanterns and candles are lit in temples and homes during this five-day feast. This is also the time of New Year on the Newari calendar.

Bala Chaturdasi, in November or December, centers around Pashupatinath Temple, on the Bagmati River east of Kathmandu. This temple, dedicated to Shiva in the form of Pashupati (Lord of the Animals), is the holiest of Hindu shrines. Pilgrims from far away come to the festival to sprinkle grain on the temple grounds, to pray for their dead, and to bathe in the holy Bagmati River. Hindus also honor Shiva here during the great Maha Shivaratri festival in February or March.

Children begin learning the alphabet during Basanta Panchami, the January-February festival dedicated to Sarasvati, goddess of learning. During Ghode Jatra, in March or April, the Newars carry images of Mahadeva and other mother goddesses through the streets.

In Khumbu, the Mani Rimdu festival is held at the Tibetan Buddhist monasteries of Thyangboche (October) and Thame

In some parts of Nepal, special swings are built for use during the Dasain festival (left). Tij Brata is a fasting festival for women, during which they bathe in the Bagmati River (right).

(May). Sherpas come from miles around to witness this dramatic reenactment of Buddhism's triumph over the evil demons of the ancient Bon religion. Wearing spectacular masks, the monks retell the familiar story through music, dance, and exaggerated gestures.

CUSTOMS, MANNERS, AND MORALS

To understand "good manners" in Nepal is to understand Hindu-based concepts of ritual purity. The left hand is considered unclean. Handshaking is always done with the right hand, for instance. One should never extend the left hand in greeting. Similarly, people touch and eat food only with the right hand.

The quest for merit is a central part of Tibetan Buddhism, which has a strong influence in the highlands of Nepal. At the

Left: A dancer in a Nepalese folk dance performance.
Above: Homes as well as public buildings are often adorned with intricate carvings.

same time, each person is responsible to the community. The people of one household may have a ritual exchange of gifts with another household and pledge trust to each other. In some Sherpa villages, there are mediators who help to settle disputes between villagers.

ARTS AND CRAFTS

The Nepalese use their arts as an expression of their deeply religious outlook. Hindu and Buddhist deities and symbols appear in architecture, painting, statues, jewelry, and everyday utensils.

Nepal's earliest art styles were imported from India. The emperor Asoka built many stupas and monasteries using Indian craftsmen.

A wall of hand-made masks for sale in Durbar Square. Although masks were originaly made for religious purposes, they are now sold as souvenirs.

Eventually, the Nepalese developed their own unique style. The various types of craftspeople came to have their own classes and castes and to live in designated sections of cities. Newari artisans introduced their bronze- and wood-carving crafts into Tibet.

The Licchavi and Malla kings were Nepal's greatest art patrons. They built fabulous, ornate temples and palaces and commissioned countless religious paintings and statues. Scrolls of painted-silk Buddhist manuscripts, called Thangkas, show traditional painting styles.

Nepalese craftspeople today work in metal, stone, terra-cotta, and wood. Most of the metalwork, such as statues, is bronze. Thimi is Nepal's pottery center. Thimi potters make terra-cotta plant pots shaped like elephants, rhinos, and temple lions. Newars excel in centuries-old wood and metal crafts. In every marketplace are pots and jars made of hand-beaten copper and brass. Patan is noted for its traditional jewelry and metalwork. Weavers of Jawalkhel produce handmade carpets with Tibetan designs. Wood

Even in cities, food may be hung out under the roof to dry (left). In rural areas, animal dung is dried in round pats for use as fuel in cooking and heating (above).

carvers in Bhaktapur make replicas of temple carvings.

The Nepalese government is very protective of the nation's art treasures. Taking objects more than one hundred years old out of the country is against the law.

FOOD AND DRINK

The Nepalese people ordinarily eat two meals a day—one in the late morning and one just after sunset. Rice is the staple food throughout the country, providing about 90 percent of a person's daily calorie intake. *Daal bhat* is the most common rice preparation. In a typical meal, each diner has a bowl or plate of *bhat* (rice), pours *daal* (lentil gravy) over it, adds *tarkkaari* (steamed vegetables), and maybe mixes in a bit of *achaar* (spicy chutney). Once everything is mixed together, chunks are grasped and eaten

Goats are kept as a source of milk at this house in eastern Nepal

with the right hand, the left hand being considered unclean. After a meal, the hands are washed with water from a washing pot. The common drink is *chay,* or milk-tea, made of black tea boiled with milk and sugar.

Meat—chicken, goat, or water buffalo—is generally eaten only on special occasions or during festivals. Devout Hindus, however, do not eat beef, and the strictest Hindus eat no meat at all. Muslims abstain from pork.

Masala—herbs and spices such as cumin, coriander, turmeric, and chilies—adds a tangy flair to meat or rice dishes. *Chapati* and *puri* (flat breads) are made from the flour of various grains.

Between meals, the Nepalese enjoy any number of snacks. *Momo* is a Tibetan dumpling similar to ravioli. *Chiura* is rice pounded into a flat cake, eaten plain or roasted, often with yogurt. Then there are sweets such as *julebi,* a deep-fried sweet pastry, and *sel roti,* a deep-fried ring of rice flour.

Different regions have their own variations and specialties. For

Sherpas and other people in the high mountain regions, potatoes are the staple food instead of rice. *Rigi jur* are the Sherpas' crisp, fried potato pancakes, eaten with cheese or a dollop of yak butter. Another common highland food is *tsampa,* roasted flour made from wheat, barley, or millet—whichever is the locally available grain. *Dhiro,* another common food in the hill region, is a mushy mixture of flour and vegetables.

Milk from yaks, cows, and water buffaloes is made into a delightful variety of dairy products. Yogurt, *ghee* (clarified buffalo-milk butter), *mahi* (buttermilk), and *chhurpi* (dried cheese) are a few examples. Milk is so abundant, in fact, that there are quite a number of cheese factories in Nepal, both government-run and privately owned.

THE NEPALESE AT WORK

About 93 percent of the Nepalese people make their living by farming. Rice is the most important crop. It is cultivated in paddies, or fields submerged in shallow water.

Some Nepalese work in small mills that process rice, jute, sugar, and oilseeds. Others work at producing cigarettes, textiles, carpets, cement, and bricks. Merchants sell in stores, small shops, and market stalls. In cities and other areas that draw tourists, many people find employment in hotels and restaurants. Hardy tribespeople in mountainous regions find work as guides and porters for climbers and hikers.

There are many expert craftspeople in Nepal who are keeping centuries-old techniques and traditions alive. They include metal-workers, woodworkers, stonecutters, and sculptors. The Newars of

Patan are known for their work with metal, particularly bronze. Tibetans in Nepal use their carpet-making expertise to weave both traditional and modern designs.

Varied occupations in Nepal: top left, a rickshaw driver waiting for business; bottom left, a rural tailor, who travels with his sewing machine; and, below, a seller of roosters in the open market

Chapter 5

THE EARLY KINGDOMS

What we know of Nepal's earliest times comes from many different sources. Ancient Nepalese chronicles such as the *Swayambhunath Purana* and the *Vamsavali* mix fact with legend. They may mention an actual, historical king. But they embellish his exploits with myth to make sure his glory is preserved for future readers. We get more reliable information from records of important events or royal proclamations that were etched into metal plates or carved into stone pillars or slabs. Later records were written on palm leaves. Archeologists have unearthed artifacts from palaces whose days of glory ended more than a dozen centuries ago.

Little is known about prehistoric Nepal. Hindu and Buddhist legends tell of an ancient people who thrived in the Himalayan region when a lake still covered the Kathmandu Valley. Actually, the earliest inhabitants of Nepal were primitive humans called *Orepithecus*. Occupying the hills of Nepal perhaps a million years ago, they were organized into tribes and used simple tools.

THE KIRATI

Nepal's earliest kingdoms flourished in the Kathmandu Valley and the Terai. Some Mongolian and some Indo-Aryan tribes

The legendary village of Lalitpur, founded about A.D. 299, became today's central Nepalese city of Patan.

settled in the region. In historic times the first people known to have lived in Nepal were a Mongolian tribe called the Kirati. They are believed to have invaded the eastern Terai in the seventh or eighth century B.C. Rai and Limbu people of eastern Nepal are their descendants. The Kirati pushed westward into the Kathmandu Valley as far as Lalitpur (present-day Patan), which they made their center of operation. Gradually they extended their influence over other peoples in the Kathmandu Valley. The epic Indian chronicle Mahabharata tells of a Kirati king who fought in a great battle.

Among the scattered settlements and kingdoms south of Lalitpur was Lumbini, near Nepal's present-day border with India. Here, in 563 B.C., Prince Siddhartha Gautama was born. He was to become the Enlightened One, the Buddha, the founder of Buddhism. Gautama journeyed throughout India and the Kathmandu Valley preaching his philosophy of selflessness and right living.

The Asoka Pillar at Lumbini, erected by Indian emperor Asoka to mark his sojourn to Buddha's birthplace, is a holy destination for traveling Buddhist monks.

ASOKA

In the third century B.C., a fierce Indian emperor named Asoka converted to Buddhism after a gruesome battle. He became an ardent preacher of Buddha's teachings. Asoka is honored as the one who brought Buddhism to Nepal. With his daughter, Carumati, he traveled to Buddha's birthplace in Lumbini, where he erected a memorial tower. He journeyed on to the Kathmandu Valley, where he bathed in the Bagmati River. In Patan, the princess Carumati married a Kirati prince. Asoka's own son is said to have become a Buddhist monk, and many Buddhist monasteries in Nepal are credited to Asoka's missionary fervor. Legend tells that Asoka built the five great stupas that stand in Patan. A tower in Patan bears an inscription said to have been left by Asoka.

Meanwhile, a thriving culture was underway in the

Kathmandu Valley under the Kirati kings. Merchants from the valley carried on a booming trade with India to the south. As early as the fourth century B.C., Indian writings tell of fine Nepalese trade goods—carpets, blankets, yaks' tails, copper, and iron. The Nepalese also were developing their own styles of art and architecture. Buddhist monasteries and stupas, painted wooden houses, and ornate stone sculptures were to be seen in every town.

Over the years, the Kirati's influence weakened. Other tribes moved through the region, weaving new ethnic and religious threads into Nepal's cultural fabric. With the new arrivals came Hinduism, which had been the religion of India long before the time of Buddha. Out of this mix of people grew the Newars, who are still the dominant people of the Kathmandu Valley today.

Somavashis, pushing north from India, lived in the Kathmandu Valley in the first three or four centuries A.D. They introduced the four-tiered Hindu caste system and refurbished many of the valley's Hindu shrines.

THE LICCHAVI DYNASTY

In the fourth century A.D., invaders called the Licchavi swept into the Kathmandu Valley from northern India. Under the Licchavis, Hinduism, its caste system, and its social customs became firmly entrenched in Nepal. Various chronicles and stone inscriptions tell of the Licchavi dynasty's deeds. One of the earliest records is an inscription in the Changu Narayan Temple, written in A.D. 467. It identifies the Licchavi king Manadeva as the one who built the temple.

Under the Licchavis, mountain passes to the kingdom of Tibet were opened. Then Nepalese merchants were able to travel northward with their trade goods. Arts and religious ideas crossed the Himalayas, too. The Kathmandu Valley became not only a commercial center but also an intellectual and cultural center. Ideas from both north and south intermingled there, and literature, spirituality, and decorative arts flourished. The Licchavis encouraged the study of Sanskrit and ancient Indian literature. Buddhist pilgrims, teachers, and monks converged on the valley, too. Monasteries became centers of learning in which devout scholars compiled, studied, and translated lengthy volumes on Buddhist philosophy and moral codes.

Dominance in the Kathmandu Valley shifted from the Licchavis to the Thakuris in the seventh century A.D. The Licchavi king, Shevadeva, married his daughter to Amsuvarman, a Thakuri noble, who declared himself king in A.D. 605 when his father-in-law died.

Soon Nepal and China began exchanging diplomatic missions. The Chinese emissary Wang Hsuan Tse wrote of Kathmandu's dazzling palace and the king's lavish store of gold and precious stones. Hsuan Tsang, a Chinese pilgrim, wrote of "Ni-po-la" in A.D. 637. He told that the people of the Kathmandu Valley were "of a hard and savage nature," though they were excellent artists. Even then, the Newars of the valley were known for their fine craftsmanship. Chinese kings asked Newar architects to build their first pagodas.

King Amsuvarman strengthened his ties with the lands to the north when he married his daughter Bhrikuti to the king of Tibet. According to tradition, Bhrikuti and the king's Chinese wife introduced Buddhism to Tibet and converted the king to Buddhism.

A Buddhist monk studying at the monastery of Thyangboche in the Everest region. Thyangboche burned down in 1989.

Buddhists honor both wives—Green Tara (Bhrikuti) and White Tara—as goddesses.

Historical records for the next few centuries are scanty. Nobles squabbled with their kings, and local rulers throughout the valley set up smaller kingdoms of their own. Dominance among the tribes shifted this way and that. When Muslims swept through India in the eleventh century, many people of northern India fled into Nepal. Out of this wave of newcomers arose the dynasty that was to rule Nepal for more than five hundred years. By about A.D. 1200 three kingdoms dominated the Kathmandu Valley—Kantipur (Kathmandu), Lalitpur (Patan), and Bhaktapur. Just east of the valley was a fourth kingdom, Banepa. Their constant skirmishes weakened the region and paved the way for the Malla kings.

THE MALLA DYNASTY

The first king of the Malla dynasty was Arideva. Around 1200, he established himself as a leader and peacemaker in the valley. It is said that Arideva gave his son the name *Malla*—Sanskrit for "wrestler"—because he was wrestling when the newborn child was first brought to him.

The greatest of the Malla kings was Jayasthiti Malla, who reigned from 1382 to 1395. An orthodox Hindu, Jayasthiti began his political career when he married the princess of Bhaktapur. Before long, he had subdued the entire Kathmandu Valley. Then he set to work laying the foundations of today's Hindu state. One cannot help marveling at the astounding complexity of his principles —and at the fact that many have survived to this day.

Jayasthiti declared himself to be a reincarnation of the Hindu god Vishnu. Even now, this is the traditional belief regarding Nepal's kings. On the advice of Brahman priests, Jayasthiti codified an elaborate system of castes and subcastes. Brahman priests made up the highest caste. Second were warriors, which included the valley's ruling families. The lesser nobility fell into various subcastes under them. Beneath all of those, the Newars of the valley were organized into sixty-four professional castes. Of these, the lowest were the "untouchables"—butchers, blacksmiths, shoemakers, and sweepers.

Under the rule of Jayasthiti and his son and grandson, the kingdom flourished as a center of arts and culture. This period of unity, prosperity, and order ended with the death of the grandson, Yaksha Malla, in 1482. Yaksha divided the kingdom among his daughter and three sons, resulting once again in rival principalities:

A bronze statue of Malla king Narendra stands on a pillar in front of a temple in Patan (left). This temple (above) on the Durbar Square in Patan, is one ornate result of the Period of the Three Kingdoms.

Kantipur (Kathmandu), Lalitpur (Patan), Bhadgaon (Bhaktapur), and Banepa. Banepa later merged with Bhadgaon.

THE PERIOD OF THE THREE KINGDOMS

Descendants of the Malla siblings quarreled with one another until the dynasty's end. Two cousin kingdoms would ally themselves against the third, then all three would declare mutual friendship with great fanfare. But before long, another pair would gang up on the third, and on and on for almost three hundred years.

Fighting consumed much of the Mallas' resources and time. But fortunately for Nepal, the three kingdoms often worked out their rivalries through artistic display. Each king competed with the others to have the most splendid plaza, or Durbar Square, in front of his royal palace. (*Durbar* is a Persian word for "court" and applies to places where assemblies can take place.) Around the squares rose a dazzling array of temples, pagodas, obelisks, and shrines. Within the fabulous palace complexes were courtyards, gardens, gazebos, and pools. This was a golden age for Nepalese architecture and art. Rival Malla kings enlisted the finest architects, painters, sculptors, stonecutters and metalworkers they could find for these grand spectacles. They also vied for the lucrative Tibetan trade, as well as the privilege of minting Tibet's silver coins. Tibetan kings invited Nepalese artisans into their kingdom, too. An entire community of Newar craftsmen lived and worked in Lhasa, the capital of Tibet.

One notable king from this period was Siddhi Narasimba Malla (1618-1661). He made his mark in construction, building some twenty-four hundred houses throughout Patan. One day Siddhi embarked on a religious pilgrimage and was never seen again. Who knows what he might have accomplished if he had continued his reign.

Another distinguished king was Pratap Malla of Kathmandu, who ruled from 1640 to 1674. Quite a literary man, he named him-self *Kavindra*, "King of Poets," and was reputed to be proficient in fifteen languages. His crowning work was a poetic prayer to the goddess Kali, which he had engraved on a stone plaque in fifteen tongues.

Bhupatendra Malla ascended to the Bhadgaon throne in 1696. It is a wonder that he lived long enough to come to power. When he was a baby, his jealous stepmother ordered her thugs to kill him because she wanted her own son to be king. But the would-be murderers lost heart and left him in the woods, where a carpenter

Nyatapola Temple in Bhadgaon, created by Bhupatendra in the early 1700s

found him and brought him up. One day when Bhupatendra was in the royal city, the king recognized him as his long-lost son. He welcomed the young man into the royal palace and restored all the honor and wealth that was rightfully his. Among Bhupatendra's contributions as king are Bhadgaon's Nyatapola Temple and the Palace of Fifty-Five Windows.

Countless other buildings and flamboyant works of art mark the Mallas' days of glory. Unfortunately, though, their incessant competition distracted the Mallas from their most lethal enemy.

A new factor entered the history of Nepal when Prithvi Narayan Shah saw the Kathmandu Valley in 1742 and swore he would take control of the valley and its people.

Chapter 6

UNITY WITHOUT PEACE

While the Malla kings squabbled, warrior-princes to the west and east of the Kathmandu Valley were occupied with conquests of their own. By the second half of the eighteenth century, they had carved out many small, independent kingdoms throughout the hills. Among the warlords, one shining star was Prithvi Narayan Shah. Head of the Shah Dynasty in the principality of Gorkha, Prithvi became Gorkha's king in 1742.

PRITHVI AND THE MALLAS' DEMISE

Once Prithvi spied the sumptuous, shimmering Kathmandu Valley from atop a high mountain pass, he vowed to make it his. He waged his first assault in 1744 on Nuwakot, along an important caravan route for Tibetan trade. In a quarter-century of shrewd military tactics, Prithvi cut off the valley's trade and transportation routes, surrounded the valley, and fortified strategic hills. The Newars bravely defended the hilltop stronghold of Kirtipur in the southeast through two long sieges. But Prithvi and his Gorkha troops took the hill in 1766 on the third try. At last he had penetrated the valley.

The Malla kings awoke from their petty concerns too late to save their domains. When Prithvi marched into Kathmandu in

September 1768, the festival of Indra Jatra was in full swing. The whole city was caught up in revelry and drink. When the time came for the traditional anointing of the king's forehead with tika to confirm his next year in office, Prithvi himself sat upon the throne. The Kumari—a little girl venerated as the reincarnation of a goddess—affixed the sacred mark to Prithvi's head. The Mallas' fate was sealed. Prithvi easily toppled the three kingdoms, and in 1769 he deposed the last of the Malla kings. With Kathmandu as his capital, Prithvi unified the states of the Kathmandu Valley. Thus was born the Gorkha Kingdom, the foundation of modern Nepal.

THE SHAH DYNASTY

Prithvi Narayan Shah pursued a strict policy of isolationism, excluding Europeans from entering his kingdom. He was especially opposed to missionaries. He forecast nothing but trouble: "First the Bible, then trading stations, then the cannon." Prithvi and his descendants embarked on many wars of conquest to extend the kingdom's borders. Prithvi himself had hoped to conquer Tibet, but he died before he could do so. Succeeding Shah kings marched their troops far beyond the Kathmandu Valley. Gorkha warriors expanded east to present-day Sikkim and west toward Kashmir. Next they targeted the fertile Terai region to the south, then pushed onward into India.

In time, however, the Shah Dynasty began to lose its grip on the newly unified nation. Royal murders left behind child kings for whom power-hungry regents ruled. In 1795 nineteen-year-old Rana Bahadur Shah stabbed his regent and took the throne, only

Hanuman Dhoka Palace is the Old Palace in central Kathmandu. The name means "Gate of Hanuman," who is the Hindu monkey god.

to be stabbed to death by his own brother, Bhim Sen Shah. Bhim Sen made himself prime minister and regent for his infant nephew, Rajendra Bikram Shah. Continuing the dynasty's policy of expansion, he hammered away at the Indian border.

Kings of the Indian Mughal Dynasty had had India in their grip for almost six centuries. By this time, however, the Mughal Empire had weakened. Traders of the British East India Company took this opportunity to set up trading posts and fortifications in India. From there they could cash in on the rich trade with the

An old woodcut of the residence of a British envoy to Kathmandu in the 1850s

East. The pearls, silks, and other trade items brought handsome profits back in Europe.

The two forces, Nepal and the British, were bound to clash. From 1814 to 1816, Bhim Sen Shah's twelve thousand troops, many armed with only bows and arrows, battled the British and Indian armies along the Indian border. The British won. After the 1816 peace treaty, signed at Segauli, Nepal and Great Britain became allies. The British army took many stout volunteers and recruits from the defeated Gorkha Kingdom. These men formed Great Britain's famous Gurkha regiments.

THE BRAVEST OF THE BRAVE

The Gurkhas do not represent one Nepalese tribe or ethnic group, but many. Their beginnings go back to the hill people of Gorkha who helped conquer the Kathmandu Valley. Tribesmen from the valley stepped forward to help Prithvi fight the British in 1763. Other tribesmen joined their ranks as the king waged more battles on many fronts. By the time of the 1814 war with Britain, the fighters the British called "Gurkhas" consisted mainly of soldiers from the Magar, Gurung, and Thakuri tribes of the central hills and the Rai and Limbu people of the eastern Terai.

The British were impressed by these warriors, whom they found to be fierce in battle, yet of a gentle nature off the field. Gurkha units served so bravely that they became legend. The British Bishop Stortford echoed the feelings of many a British officer when he wrote of the Gurkhas: "Uncomplaining you endure hunger and thirst and wounds. . . . Bravest of the brave, most generous of the generous, never had country more faithful friends than you."

THE RULE OF THE RANAS

When Rajendra Bikram Shah grew up and took his throne, he removed his former regent from the office of prime minister. But Rajendra's treacherous and unfaithful wife sent the Shah Dynasty into ruin. In September 1846 her lover was murdered. With the help of Jang Bahadur Rana, an officer of the royal guard, she assembled five hundred noblemen in the Kot, or royal assembly hall, and demanded to know who was responsible for the murder. Gunfire erupted, leaving dozens of noblemen dead.

Jang Bahadur declared himself prime minister and gave himself the title "His Majesty the Maharaja." He exiled the king and queen to India and installed their young son in the palace. The office of prime minister, he decreed, would now be hereditary. This assured that Jang Bahadur and his relatives and descendants would continue to control Nepal—and they did, for 104 years. As for the young king, he became a virtual prisoner in his own palace.

Although Jang Bahadur's move was treacherous, the rule of the Ranas did bring much-needed stability to the country.

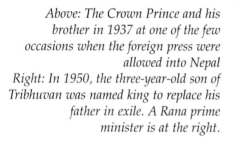

Above: The Crown Prince and his brother in 1937 at one of the few occasions when the foreign press were allowed into Nepal
Right: In 1950, the three-year-old son of Tribhuvan was named king to replace his father in exile. A Rana prime minister is at the right.

Realizing how important foreign relations were, Jang paid an official visit to Queen Victoria of England. A later Rana ended slavery in Nepal in 1926 by spending millions of rupees to purchase the slaves' freedom. He also outlawed the custom of *sati*, in which a widow was expected to throw herself on her husband's funeral pyre and burn to death. In general, though, the Ranas paid little attention to public education and health.

The Ranas closed Nepal to outsiders, particularly to visitors from the West. This protected Nepal from becoming a colony of one of the superpowers of the time, such as Great Britain, but it kept Nepal from buying and selling goods outside its borders.

Over the years, the Rana family grew in numbers. Jang

The new Narayanhiti Royal Palace and a palace guard (inset)

Bahadur himself had fathered more than one hundred children. By the 1920s there were so many Ranas—all expecting high positions —that the prime minister felt he had to rank them. There were A-, B-, and C-Ranas, with privileges clearly outlined in descending order. B-Ranas, for instance, were limited to palaces of no more than seventy rooms and could never be prime ministers. C-Ranas could live in large villas but could never be generals. Prime Minister Padma Shamsher tried to introduce free elections and a new constitution in 1948, but A-Ranas forced him to resign. Agitation among disgruntled C-Ranas helped pave the way for the return of the Shahs.

Nepal's king, Tribhuvan, as he arrived by air from a brief exile in India (above). His exile in 1950 was brought about by disagreements with the Rana prime minister. His return in 1951 signaled a new era for Nepal, when democratic elections, as evidenced by the ballot counting seen at left, became possible and the country's borders were opened to the outside world.

Chapter 7

EXPERIMENTS WITH DEMOCRACY

In 1950 the king, Tribhuvan, fled to India, aided by the Indian government and by the Nepalese living in India. From there he managed to gather resistance forces to revolt against the Rana government. Meanwhile, the Nepalese in India and anti-Ranas in the Kathmandu Valley had formed the Nepali Congress Party (NCP). They led the Nepalese in rising up against the Ranas and toppling their regime.

THE RETURN OF THE SHAHS

With the Ranas' grip on the country broken at last, the Shahs' power was restored. In 1951 Tribhuvan returned in triumph, removed the Rana prime minister, and set up a constitutional monarchy. After years of isolation, the ban on foreign visitors was lifted. Travelers from the West were finally welcome to visit Nepal.

Over the next few years, the heads of various political parties often held the post of prime minister and led the government. At other times the king himself functioned as head of state. King Tribhuvan had hoped to establish a parliamentary system of government in Nepal, similar to Great Britain's. However, he did not live long enough to see this through. On Tribhuvan's death in 1955, his son, Mahendra, succeeded him.

King Mahendra accepted his father's vision of a parliamentary government for Nepal. In February 1959, he enacted Nepal's first constitution, modeled after those of India and Great Britain. It provided for a National Assembly, similar to Britain's Parliament. The Assembly had an upper house and a lower house, with members of the lower house to be elected by popular vote. Shortly thereafter, Nepal held the first democratic elections in its history, to select assembly members. The majority of the seats went to members of the Nepali Congress Party, and party leader, B.P. Koirala, became prime minister and leader of the government.

Nepal's new government lasted barely a year. King Mahendra accused Koirala and his Nepali Congress Party of being corrupt and ineffective. In December 1960 the king suspended the constitution, dissolved the parliament, sent Koirala and his government out of power, and declared himself the only ruler of Nepal. Koirala was charged with treason.

THE PANCHAYAT PERIOD

Mahendra came to believe that Nepal's government should be more "Nepalese"—not just a reflection of the government of a foreign land. On December 16, 1962, he issued a new constitution that allowed for no political parties. Instead, there was to be a nationwide system of assemblies, or *panchayats*. Each village would elect members to its own panchayat, as would each town and each district in the country. At the top of the hierarchy was the

Left: The coronation of King Mahendra, walking beneath a golden umbrella, in 1956
Right: King Birendra Bir Bikram Shah Dev and his queen Aishwarya riding a painted elephant in his coronation parade in 1975

National Parliament, or Rastriya Panchayat. The king would appoint the prime minister. (Mahendra himself served as prime minister one year.) In time, this system settled into place. Gradually, Mahendra reestablished friendly relations with leaders of the old political parties.

KING BIRENDRA

King Mahendra suffered a heart attack and died in January 1972. His twenty-seven-year-old son, Birendra Bir Bikram Shah Dev, tenth ruler of the Shah Dynasty, ascended to the throne. The

Residents of Pokhara voting for district officials under the watchful eye of a Nepalese soldier

new King Birendra continued his father's support for the panchayat system. In 1979 antigovernment demonstrators demanded a change in the way Nepal was ruled, but they were brutally quashed. As opposition continued Birendra gave in and agreed to hold a national referendum. The Nepalese were to vote on which style of government they wanted: they could keep the panchayat system or return to the multiparty parliamentary style.

The May 1980 referendum favored the panchayats, by a narrow majority of 54.8 percent. Keeping the spirit of reform, King Birendra amended the constitution to give the Rastriya Panchayat more power and to allow its members to be elected by popular vote. The May 1981 election for assembly members was the first since 1959.

This time, however, things did not settle down peaceably. The 1982 Press Act tightened censorship of the press. A late monsoon season brought about droughts and food shortages. Though political parties were still outlawed, the Nepali Congress Party held a convention in 1985. Members agreed to use acts of civil disobedience to push for a multiparty system and parliamentary rule, but this campaign ended after some extremist groups began setting off bombs. The Rastriya Panchayat reacted by passing strict antiterrorist laws.

To reshuffle the strife-torn government, a general election was called in 1986. About two-thirds of the legislators were replaced, and there was a new prime minister and council of ministers. The government was still trying to clean up its image of being corrupt. In a 1987 anticorruption drive, several top government officials were removed on drug-smuggling charges. To make the government more efficient, departments were reorganized and more than 160 officials were fired.

Meanwhile, the Nepali Congress Party was gaining wider support. Left-wing factions such as the Communist Party of Nepal (CPN) were growing, too. At the same time the government was cracking down even harder on party leaders and political gatherings. In November 1988 the NCP and several other groups met in Kathmandu. Their talks led to the formation in February 1990 of the Movement for the Restoration of Democracy (MRD).

The MRD's stated aims were to improve Nepal's economic conditions, restore democracy, change the absolute monarchy to a constitutional one, legalize political activities, and introduce a multiparty political system. As expected, the government tried to prevent the MRD's development by tightening censorship and arresting activists.

Weeks of police confrontations, violent demonstrations, mass arrests, and labor strikes ensued. On April 5 the prime minister resigned. King Birendra immediately dissolved his council of ministers and launched an inquiry into the twenty deaths that occurred as a result of the riots. But the very next day troops fired on a huge crowd of demonstrators outside the royal palace, and fifty people were killed. Arrests and curfews followed, but this time Birendra sat down to serious talks with his opponents. He

When the police fired on prodemoc-racy demonstrations in April 1990, they killed a number of people, including this girl's friend, whose photograph she is decorating.

ended up abolishing the panchayat system, lifting the ban on political parties, and freeing political and religious prisoners

A NEW STYLE OF GOVERNMENT

A temporary government was formed until national elections could be held. It consisted of the two major opposition groups: the Nepali Congress Party and the United Left Front (ULF), a new party composed of several Communist and labor factions. A Constitutional Recommendation Commission began the task of drafting a new constitution. Among other things, it provided for a bicameral, or two-house, parliament, with members of the House of Representatives elected by popular vote.

Finally, on May 12, 1991, national elections were held. The NCP won 110 of the 205 seats in the new House of Representatives, and party secretary Girija Prasad Koirala became prime minister. Eighty-six seats went to Communist and labor groups, now merged to form the Communist Party of Nepal (United Marxist Leninist)—CPN (UML). Many of those votes came from the eastern hills and the Terai.

Nepal's new style of government did not bring peace and

Two Nepalese boys enjoy ice cream in front of a wall covered with posters for the first free election in many years, in 1991. The boy on the right has the symbol of the Communist Party on his forehead.

harmony. Prime Minister Koirala faced constant criticism from NCP leaders, who found him too conservative. In 1992 Communist and other opposition groups organized strikes and demonstrations because of rising prices, water shortages, and government corruption. Police were called out to control the violent mobs, and several people were killed. In 1993 two top UML leaders were mysteriously killed. When a government inquiry ruled that their deaths were accidental, there were nation-wide protests. Meanwhile, King Birendra tried to find honorable places for officials who had served under the old panchayat system by appointing many of them to his Council of State.

Beset by serious divisions within the NCP leadership, Prime Minister Koirala resigned in 1994. The king considered dissolving the Parliament, and new elections were called. As sure as the seasonal monsoons, demonstrations once again swept the country.

After elections were held in November 1994, the winning UML formed a new government.

Above: The king and queen during an Indra Jatra festival
Below: Harvest time in Kathmandu Valley

Chapter 8

GOVERNMENT
AND THE ECONOMY

GOVERNMENT

Nepal's system of government is known as a constitutional monarchy. The king, Birendra Bir Bikram Shah Dev, is the chief of state and the supreme commander of the army. The position of king is hereditary, passing through the male line. The constitution requires that the king be Hindu and an ethnic Indo-Aryan. A Nepalese king is believed to be a manifestation of the Hindu god Vishnu. However, he must operate within the bounds of Nepal's constitution. The present constitution was adopted on November 10, 1990, replacing the constitution of 1962. It guarantees certain basic human rights, lifts the ban on political parties, and abolishes the death penalty.

The king and his Council of Ministers hold the executive power. The ministers are responsible for administering and supervising the country's activities. They also advise the king in matters of state.

The prime minister is the head of government. The king appoints as prime minister a leader of the party in parliament that can obtain a majority vote within thirty days. The prime minister

*Kathmandu's City Hall (above) and the
Community Police Service, at work helping
residents and visitors (right)*

then chooses other members of the House to serve on the Council
of Ministers.

Nepal's legislature, or lawmaking body, consists of two chambers
—the 205-member House of Representatives, or Pratinidhi Sabha,
and the 60-member National Council, or Rastriya Sabhat.
Representatives are elected to five-year terms by popular vote.
National Council members serve six-year terms. The king
nominates ten of them, the House of Representatives elects thirty-
five (including three women), and the electoral college (heads of
regional committees) elects fifteen.

A chief justice and fourteen other judges make up Nepal's
Supreme Court, the nation's chief judicial body. There are two
other levels of courts: appellate courts and district courts.

Below the national level Nepal is divided into four major
development regions, fourteen administrative zones, and seventy-
five districts.

Political parties, though legalized in 1990, are required to register with the election commission. To be recognized, a party also must receive at least 3 percent of the votes for members of the House of Representatives, and 5 percent of the candidates it presents for election must be women.

Some of the major political parties are the Nepali Congress Party (NCP), the Communist Party of Nepal (United Marxist Leninist) or CPN (UML), and the National Democratic Party (NDP). There are about twenty other "communist" parties and several regional and ethnic parties, but none of these has been recognized as a national party. The NCP-CPN (UML) collaboration was responsible a new democratic constitution in which the governing principles are a constitutional monarchy and a multi-party parliamentary system.

NATIONAL ECONOMY

Nepal is one of the poorest countries in the world. The average income per person is only about $170 a year. With its rough terrain, Nepal is also one of the least-developed countries. Almost 5.5 million acres (2.2 million hectares) are snow-covered year round, making any kind of development or productivity impossible. The lack of an extensive road system through the rugged country is a major obstacle to trade.

Nepal's major industries are agriculture, manufacturing, and tourism. Agriculture is by far the most valuable economic activity. It accounts for more than half of the country's entire gross domestic product (GDP). (The GDP is the total value of a country's production in a year.) Twenty-eight percent of Nepal's land area is used for agriculture. About 93 percent of Nepalese make their

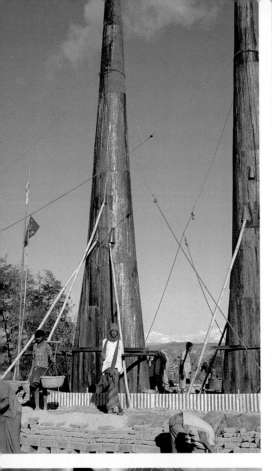

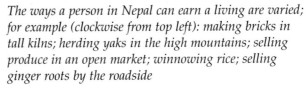

The ways a person in Nepal can earn a living are varied; for example (clockwise from top left): making bricks in tall kilns; herding yaks in the high mountains; selling produce in an open market; winnowing rice; selling ginger roots by the roadside

living at farming, raising livestock, or both. The Terai is Nepal's major farm region. Massive irrigation projects have been instituted there since 1951.

The principal crops are rice, maize (corn), barley, sugarcane, and various vegetables. Other important farm products are wheat, potatoes and other root crops, millet, lentils and other pulses (crops with edible seeds), linseed, barley, jute and other fibers, tobacco, cardamom (a spice), fruits, and oilseeds. Farmers in the Terai raise tropical fruits, cotton, and spices. Many medicinal herbs grown in the mountains bring a high price in world markets.

Cattle are Nepal's major livestock animal, followed by goats and buffaloes. All three types of animals provide meat, milk, butter, and ghee.

Nepal's major industrial activities are manufacturing, mining, and construction. Cottage industries such as basket making and fabric weaving account for about three-fifths of Nepal's industrial production. Although Nepal is not highly industrialized, it produces a number of goods by modern factory methods. These include bricks, tiles, cement, soap, textiles, clothing, jute, sugar, matches, leather, cigarettes, shoes, and chemicals. Nepalese factories also make various items to be sold as souvenirs, and many of these are exported to other countries for resale. Statues of Buddha sold in Ladakh, India, for instance, are very likely to have been made in Nepal.

The Terai's Biratnagar Jute Mills, opened in 1936, were Nepal's first industry. Today this mill is the country's largest single employer. Most of Nepal's manufacturing industries are located in the Kathmandu Valley.

Mining plays a small role in Nepal's economy. There are mica

Because elephants are used both for tourists and heavy work, elephant trainers are needed (left). Construction crews like the one shown above often include both men and women.

mines east of Kathmandu and deposits of lignite, copper, cobalt, and iron in other parts of the country. Some petroleum exploration is taking place in southeastern Nepal. In the remote northern region of Mustang, there are gold and turquoise deposits, but they are not exploited commercially.

India is Nepal's major trade partner. Most of Nepal's imported goods come from India, and India receives most of Nepal's exports. Cotton clothing, jute goods, carpets, rice, wheat, leather hides, animal and vegetable oils, and live animals are the major exports. Sal and somal are the main commercial trees, with most of the timber being exported to India. Sabrai grass is sold to India for making paper and pulp.

TRANSPORTATION

Nepal's national airline, Royal Nepal Airlines (RNAC), flies between Kathmandu and a surprising number of outlying towns.

The road into Tibet follows the steep river valley of the Bhote Kosi River.

A remote "airport," however, may be no more than a landing strip in a clearing. Early every morning, Royal Nepal also has an hour-long flight from Kathmandu north over the high Himalayas. About twenty international airlines fly to Kathmandu's Tribhuvan International Airport. Visitors to Nepal can fly in from Delhi, Benares, Calcutta, Bangkok, Rangoon, Hong Kong, Karachi, Frankfurt, Lhasa, Singapore, Patna, and Dubai.

The first car in the Kathmandu Valley belonged to a Rana prime minister. Porters carried it over the mountains, in unassembled parts, to the capital city. Kathmandu had only one road at the time, and the prime minister wanted to take a drive. There the car was put together and he went for a spin. It was not much of a drive, though; the road was only 2,625 feet (800 meters) long. Elsewhere in the country, as late as the 1950s, there were only foot trails through the mountains and villages.

Today six major roads run through Nepal, most built as cooperative efforts between Nepal and other countries. The

Transportation in Nepal includes buses that become crowded on the outside as well as inside (left), and a major international airport at which many airlines from other nations land (right)

longest is the 621-mile (1,000-kilometer) Mahendra Raj Marg. Running through the Terai, it is Nepal's segment of the Pan-Asian Highway, planned to stretch from western Turkey all the way across Asia. Engineers from Great Britain, the United States, the former Soviet Union, and India all helped build it. China helped build the so-called Chinese Road to the border of Tibet, as well as the road between Kathmandu and Pokhara. The highway from Lamosangu to Jiri is a joint Nepal-Switzerland project, and India contributed to the Tribhuvan Raj Path between Kathmandu and the Indian border.

Throughout Nepal there are more than 1,600 miles (2,575 kilometers) of paved roads. Kathmandu itself has an extensive system of roads, and a ring road encircles the Kathmandu Valley. Traffic in Nepal runs on the left-hand side of the road.

The only rail line within Nepal is a short freight line from India that ends just inside the Nepalese border. Passenger trains run through India up to the border, but there they stop. Railroad travelers who arrive at the border must then take a bus to go to Kathmandu or Pokhara.

COMMUNICATION

Nepal began its first television broadcasts in 1986. By 1991 there were about 40,000 television sets in the country. The government runs the country's one television station. However, radio communications in Nepal reach a much wider audience. About 90 percent of Nepalese hear radio broadcasts of Nepal's four AM radio stations, as well as the Voice of America, the British Broadcasting Company, some Indian and Bangladeshi stations, and Chinese broadcasts in Nepali from Tibet. They listen on an estimated 670,000 radios, so that even people in remote areas hear the news.

Nepal's 1990 constitution guaranteed freedom of the press. After that the government relaxed its heavy censorship of the printed news media. Dozens of daily and weekly newspapers, as well as a number of magazines, are published in Nepal. Most are in the Nepalese language, but several are in English. The major Nepalese daily newspaper is *Gorkhapatra*, and the official English-language daily is *Rising Nepal*.

This Nepalese man is carefully studying the newspaper pinned onto a wall to decide how he is going to vote in the upcoming election.

Durbar Square in Kathmandu, an open area of shrines, markets, and tourists

Chapter 9

PALACES, PEAKS,
AND PLAINS

Three of Nepal's largest cities lie within the Kathmandu Valley— Kathmandu, Patan, and Bhaktapur.

KATHMANDU

In the tenth century, it is said, the goddess Malakshmi appeared to King Gunakamadeva in a dream. She told him to found a new city, built in the shape of a sword, at the juncture of the Vishnumati and Bagmati rivers. Thus, according to legend, began the capital city of Kathmandu. Actually, a settlement existed there long before King Gunakamadeva's time. The city's present layout dates from the Malla kings of the sixteenth and seventeenth centuries. They commissioned much of the art, architecture, and statuary that lends the city of Kathmandu its beautiful and exotic character today.

There are a number of ways to get around the crowded streets and alleyways of Kathmandu. There are taxis; three-wheeled public scooters that can carry six passengers; canopied, two-seater rickshaws powered by hardy cyclists; and bicycles, which visitors

A family praying at a Muslim mosque in Kathmandu (left), and typical city apartment buildings (above)

can rent. Then—to best experience the sights, sounds, and smells of Kathmandu—one can walk.

The city has an old section—lower, or southern, Kathmandu—and a new section—upper, or northern, Kathmandu. There was once fierce rivalry between the two. Every year on the feast of Kumara Sastri, the warrior god, the two sides held a stone-throwing battle. Wounded losers were dragged off and sacrificed. One of the Rana prime ministers abolished this custom, though, after a British official got hit with a flying stone.

Durbar Square is the heart of old Kathmandu. There stands the old royal palace, home of Nepal's monarchs since the sixteenth- and seventeenth-century Malla kings. Within the palace walls are elegant courtyards, exquisite wood carvings, and sculptures of gods, goddesses, and demons. One of the three great sleeping Vishnu statues of the Kathmandu Valley is east of the palace compound, in the royal gardens. No visitors are allowed in the gardens, though. There are more than fifty monuments—towers, shrines, and temples—in Durbar Square, some dating back as far as the twelfth century.

Two other fascinating structures in Durbar Square are

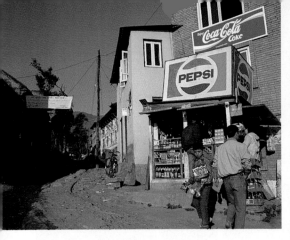

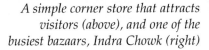
A simple corner store that attracts visitors (above), and one of the busiest bazaars, Indra Chowk (right)

Kasthamandap and Kumari Bahal. Kasthamandap is a large, open hall that once sheltered pilgrims and traders bound for Tibet. Legend holds that the original structure, built many centuries ago, was carved from the wood of a single magical tree. Its name, meaning "Pavilion of Wood," gave Kathmandu its name.

Kumari Bahal is an ornate Buddhist monastery that houses the Kumari, or living goddess. Once in a while, this little girl, believed to be the reincarnation of the Hindu goddess Kumari, can be glimpsed at her second-floor window.

"Freak Street" and "Pie Alley" are two streets running off Durbar Square. These nicknames date from the 1960s, when a wave of hippies from other countries poured into Kathmandu.

Northeast of Durbar Square is Indra Chowk. This meeting point of six streets is the setting for a lavish bazaar. Merchants here hawk various necessities and luxuries—carpets, shawls, jewelry, pottery, musical instruments, and fruits. Many sell their wares from the steps and courtyards of the square's temples and shrines: Akash Bhairab, Shiva Mandir, Jana Bahal, Kel Tol, or Chamunda.

The city's biggest bazaar is Asan Tol, at another crossroads farther north. The crunch of the crowd is so tight that only foot

Rani Pokhara, King Pratap Malla's memorial to his son for his wife, and the clock tower of Trichandra College

traffic can get through. Here, too, shoppers swarm around merchants who are camped before shrines.

Kathmandu's new section presents a striking contrast to the old town. Banks, airline offices, embassies, hotels, and travel agencies line the parallel main thoroughfares, Durbar Marg and Kanti Path. At the north end of these two streets is Narayanhiti Royal Palace, residence of the royal family. High walls and dour guards keep the public away from this magnificent eighteenth-century compound.

A few blocks south of the palace is Rani Pokhari, a great pool that King Pratap Malla built for his grieving wife in 1670 after their son died. Farther south, Ratna Park, a public gathering place, has its own little bazaar. Beyond the park the Tundikhel forms a great, grassy expanse where the king presides over military parades and other official ceremonies. In the northwest corner of the Tundikhel, the silver-eyed, black-stone statue of Mahakala is enshrined. The Tundikhel's southern end is marked by the Martyr's Gate, honoring revolutionaries who tried to oust the Ranas in 1940. The New Road, a grand boulevard built after a 1934 earthquake, stretches westward from Kanti Path toward Durbar Square. Here wealthier shoppers can buy expensive clothes and jewelry, electronics, and other high-cost imported goods.

East of the Tundikhel, at the end of Prithvi Path, is Singh Durbar. Built in 1901 by Prime Minister Chandra Shamser Rana, this palace was once the largest private residence in Asia. Its 1,700 rooms were adorned with marble columns and crystal chandeliers. It took a staff of 1,500 servants to maintain it. Nepalese government offices have been housed there since 1951. A fire in 1974 destroyed most of the complex, though the grandiose facade and many reception halls remain.

PATAN AND BHAKTAPUR

Just south of Kathmandu, on a plateau over the Bagmati River, is Patan. The third-largest city in Nepal, Patan's former name was Lalitpur, "the beautiful city," and it still has a section called Lalitpur. Patan is the Kathmandu Valley's oldest city and also its center for arts and crafts and religious architecture.

Patan's population are Newars, and the city is about equally divided between Hindus and Buddhists. Some of the main shrines are used by both religious communities. According to tradition, the Buddhist emperor Asoka and his daughter, Carumati, founded Patan in the third century B.C. To mark Patan's boundaries, they erected five stupas, one at each of the four compass points and one in the center. Actually, it is unlikely that Asoka was ever in the region. Nevertheless, the Buddhists of Patan revere these earthen mounds, called the Asoka Stupas, as symbols of their religious heritage.

Patan's two major streets intersect in the center of town. On the north side of this crossing is Durbar Square, and to the south are the shops and businesses of Mangal Bazaar. Durbar Square is home to a fabulous collection of Newari architecture, including the Royal Palace and several temples. Malla kings built the palace complex in the seventeenth and eighteenth centuries and filled it with shrines, walled gardens, elaborate gates, and temples. Its three large courtyards open into the square. One contains an ornate sunken bath called Tusha Hiti. The four-story tower of Degutale Temple, honoring the Mallas' personal goddess, rises above the complex. In front of the temple, high atop a pillar, is a sculpture of King Yoganarendra Malla.

Krishna Mandir, an architectural masterpiece, is the most stunning temple in the palace square. Built of limestone by a seventeenth-century Malla king, it features stone carvings of scenes from the great Hindu epics. South of Mangal Bazaar is the temple of Red Machhendranath, a form of the guardian god of the Kathmandu Valley. The weeks-long summer celebration of Rato Machhendranath is Patan's grandest festival.

During the Licchavi dynasty, pilgrims, monks, and students came to Patan for religious study and devotion. Monasteries were to be seen everywhere. More than 150 monastery complexes

Krishna Mandir, a temple in Patan's Durbar Square, and the Taleju Bell. Inset: Patan is famed for its fine Newar souvenir masks and delicate metalwork.

remain, although most were converted to housing for artisans in Patan's many craft guilds. But Patan still has eighteen major, active monasteries. The largest is Hiranya Varna Mahavihar, with more than 1,500 resident monks.

As early as the seventh century A.D., Newari craftsmen were widely known for their skill in casting bronze and inlaying metal with precious stones. Today Patan's Newars still excel in metalwork, jewelry, statuary, stonecutting, and other traditional crafts.

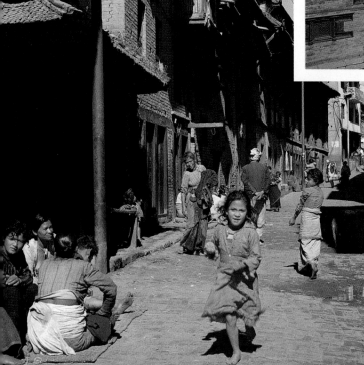

Many Tibetan refugees who live near Patan weave wonderful rugs to earn a living (top left). Patan's 400-year-old Mahabouddha Temple (top right) has thousands of terracotta images of Buddha. This Bhaktapur street (left) leads to the Palace of Fifty-Five Windows (above), which was the audience hall of a Malla king.

Outside of Durbar Square is Kumbheshwar, a five-story Hindu temple. Nepal's largest Tibetan refugee camp is in Jawalkhel, a southwest suburb of Patan. Here one can watch expert weavers at their looms, producing handmade Tibetan carpets in both traditional and modern designs.

Ten miles (16 kilometers) east of Kathmandu is the medieval city of Bhaktapur. The most imposing sight in Bhaktapur's Durbar Square is Nyatapola Pagoda, 100 feet (30 meters) high. Its doors have been locked for two hundred years, and pairs of fierce mythical beasts line the entrance stairs. One passes through the Golden Gate (actually bronze) to enter the Royal Palace, built by King Bhupatendra Malla. The palace's audience hall is called the Palace of Fifty-Five Windows.

THE EAST

Eastern Nepal is the most mountainous region of the country, with five of the world's ten tallest peaks. In the massive, jagged cluster of mountains sloping up to the Tibetan border are Everest, Lhotse I, Makalu, and Cho Oyu. In the far east, at Nepal's border with Sikkim, is Kanchenjunga. For many years, Kanchenjunga was closed to travelers. Recently, however, the travel restriction was lifted on part of the region.

The Solu and Khumbu regions are commonly linked

Mountain villagers putting food on their slate roof to dry

Trekkers at Cho La Pass in the Himalayas (left), and the village of Junbesi in Solu-Khumbu (above)

together under the name Solu-Khumbu. This is the home of the Sherpas, whose language and culture reflect their Tibetan roots. Clinging to hillsides throughout Solu-Khumbu are many Tibetan Buddhist monasteries, or *gompas*. Solu's Thupten Choling Monastery is the largest Buddhist monastery in Nepal. A reconstruction of Tibet's destroyed Rongbuk Monastery, it is the home of the spiritual leader of the Everest region.

SAGARMATHA NATIONAL PARK

Sagarmatha National Park was established in 1976, thanks to the efforts of Sir Edmund Hillary. He appealed to the Ministry of

Mount Cho Oyu, seen in the distance, from Sagarmatha National Park

Foreign Affairs of New Zealand, his home country, to help set up the park so that the area could be protected and preserved, for both the Nepalese and the rest of the world. The ministry agreed to provide funds and technical assistance for five years and to help train the Nepalese in park management. Within the 480-square-mile (1,243-square-kilometer) park are three of the world's highest peaks: Everest, Lhotse, and Cho Oyu. Some twenty-five hundred Sherpas live in Sagarmatha. It is unusual for indigenous peoples to live in any of the world's national parks.

Animals in Sagarmatha National Park are protected by law. This has increased the populations of such rare species as the Impeyan pheasant—Nepal's national bird—and the goatlike Himalayan tahr. Other animals inhabiting the park are the snow leopard, musk deer, golden eagle, and Himalayan griffon vulture. Vivid pink, red, and purple rhododendrons line the park's trails.

One of the most difficult problems facing park officials is enforcing the forest-conservation laws. Both hikers and Sherpas have stripped the slopes of bushes and trees for firewood. This deforestation caused a serious soil erosion problem. Cutting wood

A Tibetan stupa, or shrine, at Namche Bazar, the place where many Tibetan refugees entered Nepal when fleeing from the Chinese

in the park is now against the law, and hikers are required to bring their own fuel with them. But it's impossible to patrol the whole park at once, and people still manage to chop down precious young trees for an evening's firewood.

Most expeditions begin from Namche Bazar, a town nestled in a bowllike depression near the entrance to the park. Thick forests once covered the area around Namche, which was cleared for an airstrip. Once the national park was established, a massive reforestation project began. New seedlings are being planted in the hope of restoring the area's ground cover.

CENTRAL NEPAL

In almost the exact center of Nepal is the Pokhara Valley, where Pokhara is the major town. Scanning the northern horizon from the valley, one sees a stunning arc of snow-shrouded mountains. Toward the northwest, if the air is clear, Dhaulagiri is visible. The Annapurna range rises just north of the valley. A

Left: The twin "fish tail" peaks of Machhapuchare
Right: A street in Pokhara

unique point on the horizon is Machhapuchare, meaning "fish tail." Its twin peaks, less than a mile apart, look like the forked tail of a fish pointing into the sky.

A cultural blend of two broad groups of people live in the Annapurna and Pokhara Valley region. The lower-lying southern valley is home to Indian ethnic and caste groups, mostly Hindu, whose homes have mud walls and thatched roofs. In the hills to the north are Gurungs, Magars, and Thakalis. They are Hindu and Buddhist combined, and they live in whitewashed, slate-roofed homes. Many recruits for the Gurkha regiments are drawn from among these hill people, and the pensions of retired Gurkha soldiers provide the area with a certain wealth.

More than 150 inches (380 centimeters) of rain falls in the Pokhara Valley every year, watering the rice paddies and terraced grain and mustard fields. Banana and citrus trees, blooming cactuses, and other colorful subtropical vegetation thrive here.

For centuries Pokhara was a rather isolated market town, serving as a crossroads for trade between Tibet and India. Pokhara's first motor vehicle, a jeep, arrived by helicopter in 1958. Paved roads and more motor traffic followed, and tourism began to grow. Today Pokhara is the starting point for many climbers and hikers. In fact, the foothills and peaks of the Annapurna range attract three times more hikers than does the Everest region. This is partly because the government has been trying to shift climbers' interest away from Everest to ease environmental problems.

The Annapurna area became such a popular destination for tourists and climbers that its environment, too, began to suffer from deforestation and erosion. The Annapurna Conservation Area Project (ACAP) was established to protect the region. The ACAP charges entrance fees for visitors, then spends the proceeds on conservation and development projects.

The circular route around the Annapurna and adjacent Lamjung ranges is a well-established, month-long hike. On the circuit's western arc, travelers descend into the Kali Gandaki gorge, between Annapurna and Dhaulagiri. This is the deepest gorge in the world.

THE TERAI

The Terai, the strip of land along Nepal's southern border, occupies about one-fifth of the country's land area. Its average width is about 40 miles (64 kilometers), and its narrowest point is only about 10 miles (16 kilometers) wide. Yet 70 percent of Nepal's cultivable land is in the Terai, as well as almost half the population. With the Siwalik Hills forming its northern border, the Terai is Nepal's lowest-lying land area. When the rivers flood during monsoon season, they leave rich deposits of silt in the fields and rice paddies. Most of the country's agriculture and industry are located in the Terai.

Women carrying things in very different Nepalese places: on a suspension bridge across a deep gorge (left), and on a farm in the Terai (right)

Before the mid-1950s, jungles and swamps covered most of the Terai. Malaria-carrying mosquitoes were a deadly presence from April to October. Then the government began a program of spraying the Terai with the insecticide DDT. Settlers from both Nepal and India began moving in, clearing the thick, subtropical jungleland, and cultivating rice, wheat, sugarcane, oilseeds, jute, and other crops.

The people and culture of the Terai are as much related to India as they are to the rest of Nepal. Many northern Indian dialects are spoken there, as well as Nepali. Tharus are the major ethnic group, with various subgroups living all along the southern border.

In the far eastern Terai is Biratnagar, Nepal's second-largest city, which has a population of more than 100,000. It is a major industrial center, with factories and mills that produce jute, sugar, textiles, stainless steel, and timber and rice products.

Janakpur, west of Biratnagar, is believed to be the birthplace of Sita. She was the wife of Rama, an incarnation of Vishnu and the hero of the Indian epic *Ramayana*. Thousands of Hindu pilgrims

Left: Guests riding an Asian elephant at Tiger Tops in Royal Chitwan National Park
Above: Lumbini, where Buddha was born, and the pool where his mother bathed after giving birth

come to Janakpur for its two annual festivals—Sita's birthday and the wedding anniversary of Sita and Rama. They bathe in the city's sacred ponds and pray in the elaborately carved Janaki Temple.

Farther west is Royal Chitwan National Park, the most-visited site in the Terai. Counting Parsa Wildlife Reserve, an extension of the park, Royal Chitwan covers 470 square miles (1,217 square kilometers). Opened in 1973, the park was Nepal's first wildlife preserve. It had been the royal family's hunting grounds, and they were eager to protect the area from encroaching settlement and deforestation. Now, disappearing animal species are thriving again in Royal Chitwan, and various conservation projects and experiments are in progress. At the same time, lodges and resorts carry on a thriving tourist trade. Visitors ride through the grasslands, jungles, and swamps astride elephants, which they can rent for the day. Their mahout, or elephant handler, guides them to watering holes where they can see rhinoceroses, wild boars, and deer. On rare occasions, one can glimpse a tiger or a leopard. Tiger Tops is Royal Chitwan's first and best-known resort, but there are now many other resorts, lodges, and campsites throughout the park.

Southwest of Royal Chitwan National Park is Lumbini, where Prince Siddhartha Gautama—the Buddha—was born. Until 1856, Lumbini was a part of India. When the emperor Asoka visited Lumbini in 249 B.C., he erected a towering stone pillar to commemorate the holy place. But as Hinduism gained a foothold in India, Buddhism waned. Over the centuries Lumbini was neglected, and thick jungle vegetation grew over its remains. Then in 1895 a German archeologist began to excavate Lumbini's ruins. He discovered Asoka's pillar and a sandstone sculpture depicting a mythical scene of Buddha's birth from the right side of his mother, Maya Devi.

In 1968 United Nations secretary general U Thant, a devout Buddhist, visited Lumbini. He is said to have cried at the sight of the dilapidated ruins. Now an international Buddhist committee oversees Lumbini's reconstruction as a religious heritage site. Visitors can see Asoka's pillar and visit the Maya Devi temple, marking the spot where the Buddha was born. The temple houses the stone relief of Buddha's nativity. There are stupas, an Eternal Peace Flame, and two monasteries containing beautiful murals, sculptures, and statues. At Tilaurakot, 17 miles (27 kilometers) west of Lumbini, are the ruins of the palace where Prince Siddhartha grew up and lived until his enlightenment.

In the far western Terai, along Nepal's westernmost border, lies Sukla Phanta Wildlife Preserve. Among its inhabitants is the endangered blackbuck.

THE WEST

Fourteenth-century Malla kings once ruled western Nepal. This is the region west of the Kali Gandaki River—wild, sparsely populated, and the least-visited area of the country. In the far west is the Karnali River basin. Throughout western Nepal are the high, flat ridges, or *lekh*, of the lower Himalayas. The Karnali River cuts deep, forested valleys into the ridge. Except in the river valleys, the west is agriculturally poor.

Just west of the Kali Gandaki is the Baglung district. Here live the Thakalis, a Tibetan people whose special craft is handmade paper. North of Baglung, bordering Tibet, are Dolpo and Mustang. Much of Dolpo lies within Shey-Phoksumdo National Park, the largest national park in the country. Rare snow leopards roam the park, as well as blue sheep, black bears, and wolves. Dolpo's Crystal Mountain is a holy place for Tibetan Buddhists. According to legend, the mountain changed to crystal when a holy monk battled the god of the mountain and won. Many Tibetan refugees live in Dolpo, and their religious rituals blend with the natives' shamanistic rites.

Legendary Mustang used to be reachable only on foot through narrow mountain passes. Dhaulagiri peak practically seals off the

Many Tibetans, including Buddhist monks (above), live in the mountain region called Mustang. Formerly inaccessible, the mountains are now climbed by visitors with Sherpa guides to lead them. This climbers' camp (right) is at 16,000 feet (4,877 meters).

approach from the Nepal side. But now helicopter flights take passengers to Mustang and RNAC planes drop passengers in the next district, within easy walking distance. A fourteenth-century Tibetan warlord founded this kingdom—called Lo Manthang in Tibetan—and its twenty-fifth monarch still rules it. By an agreement between China and Nepal, the king can keep his position and his subjects in exchange for an annual fee of one horse and 886 rupees (about $25 United States at mid-1990 exchange rates). He reigns from the ancient city of Manthang, which is surrounded by high walls for protection. No trees grow on Mustang's barren plateau. Its eight thousand people, Tibetan-speaking Buddhists called Lopas, scratch out a few meager crops from the soil to add to their diet of yak milk and cheese.

Dolpo, Mustang, and other western regions along the Tibetan border were closed to foreign visitors in the 1960s. This was intended to prevent migration across the border and to protect travelers from Tibetan guerrilla fighters. Southern Dolpo was opened in 1989. In 1992 Mustang's capital city of Manthang was opened. Other northwestern border areas may open in time.

Jumla, the Malla kings' ancient capital, is now the jumping-off point for travel in the west. In Jumla itself, ornate temples and stone pillars remind one of the Mallas' days of glory. North of Jumla, Rara National Park is home to leopards, Himalayan black bears, and tahrs. Circled by evergreens, the park's Lake Rara lies in a high basin beneath snow-capped Gurchi Lekh. Lake Rara is Nepal's largest lake. Thakuri villages dot the route from Jumla to Rara.

Khaptad National Park, west of the Karnali River, is both a holy site and a wildlife preserve. The aged Hindu guru Khaptad Baba lives and teaches in the park's devotional area. Here there are various shrines as well as the Tribeni, the spot where streams converge to form the source of the Ganges River. Barking deer and musk deer roam the surrounding grasslands and forests.

Both Hindu and Buddhist pilgrims pass through Humla, in Nepal's far northwest corner. Their destination is Tibet's Mount Kailas and Lake Mansarovar, sacred to both religions. Here, foreigners cannot travel past a certain point on the trail. Mount Kailas is believed to be the precise point where the gods enter the realm of humans. To believers, it is the holiest spot on earth and visitors are not allowed.

A mustard field in central Nepal

THE FUTURE

Political problems aside, Nepal is making progress in many areas. Aggressive programs are in place to improve education, protect the environment, expand the road system, increase farm and factory production, and control disease.

Nepal's relations with its neighbors often are tense. India is almost too powerful an ally, as it controls most of the trade routes to and from landlocked Nepal. Talks with Bhutan, a country to the east, have deadlocked over the eastern Terai's refugee camps, home to an ethnic hodgepodge of Bhutanese, as well as Nepalese from India and Bhutan. Bangladesh, to the southeast, blames its deadly monsoon floods on Nepal's water-management policies. Relations with Nepal's age-old neighbor, Tibet, become more complicated as Nepal becomes friendlier with the People's Republic of China. In recent years Nepal's border with Tibet has been opened, then closed again.

Nepal faces many challenges as it looks to the twenty-first century. After more than two thousand years of warlords and absolute monarchs, its experiment with democracy will probably remain an experiment for years to come.

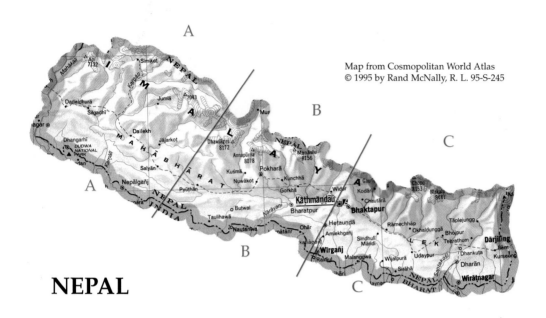

NEPAL

Amlekhgan	B	Ilan	C		
Annapurna	B	Jajarkot	A		
Bhaktapur	B	Jumla	A	Ohar	B
Bhojpur	C	Karnali (river)	A	Okhaldungga	C
Butwal	B	Kathmand(a)u	B	Pokhara	B
Chautara	B	Kodar	B	Pyuthan	B
Chopu	C	Kunchha	B	Salyan	A
Dadeldhura	A	Kusma	B	Sapta Kosi (river)	C
Dailekh	A	Mahabharat Lek (mtn)		Silgadhi	A
Dhangarhi	A		A-B	Simikot	A
Dhankuta	C	Mahakali (river)	A	Tamechhap	C
Dharan	C	Mahendranagar	A	Taplejungg	C
Dhaulagiri	B	Makalu	C	Taulihawa	B
Domolangma Feng	C	Malaggwa	C	Tebrathum	C
Dudwa Nat'l Park	A	Manaslu	B	Udaypur	C
Everest (mtn)	C	Mustang	B	Widur	B
Gaurisangkar (mtn)	B	Narayani (river)	B	Wijalpura	C
Gorkha	B	Nepalgan	A	Wiratnagar	C
Hetaunda	B	Nuwakot	B	Wirganj	B

MINI-FACTS AT A GLANCE

GENERAL INFORMATION

Official Name: Nepal Adhirajya (Kingdom of Nepal)

Capital: Kathmandu

Government: Nepal is a constitutional monarchy. The king is the chief of state and the supreme commander of the army. The king is required by law to be a Hindu and an ethnic Indo-Aryan. The king and his Council of Ministers hold the executive power. The prime minister is the head of government. The legislature consists of two chambers, the House of Representatives and the National Council. Representatives are elected for a five-year term and National Council members for a six-year term, both by popular vote. The judicial system consists of a Supreme Court, appellate courts, and district courts. For administrative purposes, the country is divided into 4 development regions, 14 administrative zones, and 75 districts.

Religion: Nepal is the only official Hindu kingdom in the world. Hinduism is the religion of 85 percent of the people, 10 percent follow Buddhism, and some 5 percent are Muslims or members of the animist religions. Many temples have both Hindu and Buddhist shrines. There still are about two dozen major active Buddhist monasteries *(gompas)* in Nepal with a large number of resident monks.

Ethnic Composition: Nepali population consists of about 35 separate ethnic groups including Gurang (known outside Nepal as Gorkhas), Limbu, Magar, Newar, Rai, Sunwar, and Yakha. The Sherpas and Thakalis, of Tibetan origin, are the tribespeople of the north. Sherpas are the most expert guides and porters in the Himalayan region.

Language: Nepali, a close relative of Hindi, is the official language. There are also some 40 other languages spoken by small ethnic groups.

National Flag: The only non-rectangular country flag in the world, it consists of two adjoining triangles in crimson (the national color of Nepal) with points at the fly; they are outlined in blue and merge at the center. A white horizontal crescent moon (the symbol of the royal family) is depicted in the upper triangle and a sun (the symbol of the Rana family) is in the lower triangle. The flag represents Nepal's hope that the country will last as long as the sun and the moon.

National Emblem: The chief elements are the national flower (the rhododendron), a white cow, a green pheasant, two Gorkha soldiers, peaks of the Himalaya mountains, the moon and the sun, the footprints of Gorakhnath (the guardian deity of the Gorkhas), and the royal headdress. At the bottom of the emblem, a red scroll carries the national motto in Sanskrit, "The Fatherland Is Worth More than the Kingdom of Heaven."

National Anthem: "Rashtriya Dhun" ("May His Majesty, Solemn and Supremely Valiant, Be Prosperous Forever")

National Calendar: Five different calendar systems are used in Nepal. The official calendar is the Vikram Samvat (lunar based) which is 57 years ahead of the Gregorian calendar. Other calendars are Newar Samvat, Shakya Samvat, Tibetan, and Gregorian.

Money: The Nepalese Rupee (NR) of 100 palsa is the official currency. In 1993 one NR was worth $0.03 in US currency.

Membership in International Organizations: Asian Development Bank (ADB); Colombo Plan; Nonaligned Movement (NAM); South Asian Association for Regional Cooperation (SAARC); United Nations (UN)

Weights and Measures: The metric system is in use, but some traditional Indian standards also are used.

Population: 1994 estimates 21,042,000 with a population density of 370 per sq. mi. (143 per sq km); 10 percent live in cities and 90 percent live in rural communities. Nepal has a large number of Tibetan refugees who live in camps, mostly near Patan.

Cities (municipalities):

> Kathmandu 419,100
> Biratnagar 130,100
> Patan 117,200
> Pokhara 95,300
> Birganj 68,800

(Population figures based on 1991 estimates.)

GEOGRAPHY

Border: Located in southeast Asia, this mountainous country is completely surrounded by land. India is to the east, south, and west, and the Tibetan Autonomous Region of China is to the north.

Land: Rectangular in shape, Nepal contains some of the most rugged and difficult mountainous landscape in the world. Nepal's three geographic regions stretch from west to east. The narrow fertile plains of Terai, occupying one-fifth of the total land area, are in the south; 70 percent of Nepal's agricultural land is in the Terai. The hill region consists of rocky foothills and lower ranges of the high Himalayas; the Kathmandu Valley is in the east-central and the Pokhara Valley is in the west-central hill region. The high Himalayas stretch some 1,550 mi. (2,500 km) in the north.

Eight of the world's ten tallest peaks rise in this region, including Mt. Everest, Dhaulagiri I, Annapurna I, and Manaslu I. In the Annapurna Range, there are 4 main peaks. Annapurna I is 26,504 ft. (8,078 m); Annapurna II is 26,040 ft. (7,937 m); Annapurna III is 24,786 ft. (7,555 m); and Annapurna IV is 24,688 ft (7,525 m). For comparison, the Sears Tower in Chicago, Illinois, is 1,454 ft. (443 m). Eighteen Sears Towers stacked on top of one another would be almost as high as Annapurna I. The Kali Gandaki Gorge between Annapurna and Dhaulagiri is the deepest gorge in the world.

Highest Point: Mt. Everest, 29,028 ft. (8,848 m)—the highest mountain in the world

Lowest Point: 230 ft. (70 m) above sea level

Rivers: Most rivers flow from north to south to meet the Ganges River system and finally empty into the Bay of Bengal. The Kosi and its seven tributaries are in the east, the Gandak system is in central Nepal, and the Karnali system is in the west. Rivers often flood during the monsoon season. Lake Rara is Nepal's largest lake.

Forests: Forests cover almost one-third of the country. Khair, sisu, somal, sal, pine, oak, rhododendron, and poplar are the trees of the southern Terai region. The lower slopes of the Himalayas are forested with spruce, fir, cypress, juniper, and birch. Above 16,000 ft. (4,877 m) only mosses, ferns, and wildflowers survive. Nepal suffers from severe deforestation and soil-erosion problems. People have stripped the land, especially slopes, of bushes and trees for firewood. A massive reforestation project is underway to restore the area's ground cover.

Wildlife: Wildlife includes hyenas, jackals, monkeys, gaur (wild oxen), deer, black and brown bears, wolves, wild sheep and goats, marmots, and musk deer. Endangered species include the snow leopard, tiger, Asian elephant, pygmy hog, Indian rhinoceros, swamp deer, and gavial. Birds include pheasants, hill partridges, flowerpeckers, sunbirds, golden eagles, and vultures.

There are several wildlife preserves and national parks. Sagarmatha National

Park has three of the world's highest peaks—Everest, Lhotse I (27,923 ft.; 8,511 m), and Cho Oyu (26,750 ft.; 8,153 m). Animals are protected and such rare species as Impeyan pheasant and Himalayan tahr have increased in number.

Climate: The climate ranges sharply (from south to north) from subtropical to arctic, with the altitude. The Terai region has hot, rainy, and cold seasons while the central hilly region has a temperate climate. The high Himalayas are covered with snow and ice all year and are bitterly cold in winter. Nepal receives 80 percent of its precipitation from summer monsoons between June and October. Over 150 in. (380 cm) of rain falls annually in the Pokhara Valley. Thunderstorms are common throughout Nepal.

Greatest Distance: North to South: 150 mi. (241 km)
East to West: 500 mi. (805 km)
Area: 56,827 sq. mi. (147,182 sq km)

ECONOMY AND INDUSTRY

Agriculture: Some 93 percent of Nepalese make their living by farming on 28 percent of the land. Fields are terraced on the mountain slopes to hold rainwater and prevent soil erosion. The principal crops are rice, maize (corn), barley, sugarcane, potatoes, wheat, millet, lentils, oilseeds, jute (for burlap, sacks, and twine), tobacco, spices, fruits, and cotton. Many medicinal plants are grown in the mountains for sale in the world market. Cattle, goats, and water buffaloes are raised for meat and milk. Sheep and goats graze the lower mountains; yaks are herded in the mountains. In winter, herds of cattle and sheep are brought down to warmer valleys.

Mining: Nepal's mineral wealth is limited. There are small deposits of mica, lignite coal, copper, limestone, garnet, cobalt, gold, turquoise, and iron ore. Wood from nearby forests supplies most of the energy consumed in the households.

Manufacturing: Small-scale factories include food-processing (rice, jute, sugar, and oilseeds), cigarettes, textiles, carpets, cement, bricks, tiles, soap, matches, leather goods, and chemicals. Cottage industries include basket making and fabric weaving.

Transportation: Nepal has a limited road system; only six major roads run through Nepal. Out of 6,000 mi. (9,600 km) of roads, some 40 percent are paved. In the mountainous region only foot trails exist. A small stretch of 33 mi. (53 km) of railroad is near the Indian border in the south. Royal Nepal Airlines (RNAC) is Nepal's national airline. The Tribhuvan International Airport is at Kathmandu. City transportation consists of taxis, three-wheeled public scooters, two-seater rickshaws, and bicycles.

Communication: Radios are the most popular means of communication. The government operates four AM radio stations. In the early 1990s, there was one radio receiver per 33 persons, one television set per 539 persons, and one telephone per 415 persons. Freedom of the press is guaranteed by the 1990 constitution. There are several Nepali and one English daily newspaper.

Trade: The chief imports are machinery and transport equipment, chemicals, petroleum, and food items. The major import sources are India, Singapore, Japan, New Zealand, China, and France. The chief export items are cotton clothing, jute goods, carpets, rice, wheat, leather hides, oils, timber, grass (for paper), and live animals. The major export destinations are India, Germany, the United States, Switzerland, Belgium, and the United Kingdom.

EVERYDAY LIFE

Health: The major diseases are malaria, diarrhea, dysentery, typhoid, cholera, leprosy, tuberculosis, hepatitis, and rabies. Life expectancy at 54 years for males and 53 years for females is low. The infant mortality rate at 98 per 1,000 is very high. Nepal has a severe shortage of doctors and hospitals. There are about one doctor and four hospital beds for every 20,000 persons.

Education: Public schools are free and five years of primary education is compulsory. Secondary school is for five years. Tribhuvan University is at Kathmandu and Mahendra Sanskrit University is in Beljhundi. In the early 1990s, the literacy rate was about 40 percent. With increased government efforts, most of the villages now have access to at least a primary school.

Holidays:	Prithvi Jayanti (National Unity Day), January 11
	Independence Day, February 18
	Nepalese New Year, mid-April
	Constitution Day, November 9
	Constitution Day, December 15
	National Day (King's Birthday), December 28

Hindu religious holidays (such as Shivratri, Holi, Baishakh Purnima, Durga Ashtami, and Deepawali) are based on the lunar calendar and may fall on different dates every year.

Culture: Pashupatinath Temple in Kathmandu, dedicated to Shiva, is the holiest of Hindu shrines. Hindu and Buddhist details and symbols appear in architecture, painting, statues, jewelry, furniture, and everyday utensils. Nepalese craftspeople work in metal, stone, terra-cotta, wood, and wool. The Nepalese cultural heritage is a source of great pride for the Nepalese.

Society: Hindus follow the caste system of Brahmans, Chhetris, Vaisyas, and Sudras. Reincarnation is a central doctrine of Hindu society. The Buddhists follow Four Noble Truths and the Eightfold Path of Buddha. Colorful masks play an important role in Buddhist religious rituals. The shamanistic healer or *jhankri* is a popular person in villages and rural areas.

Dress: Clothing is colorful. Women in rural areas wear loose blouses and long skirts. Most men wear pants and shirts, but some wear knee-length robes and tight pants. In cities women wear saris and shawls.

Housing: Most of the rural houses are small two-story structures of stone or mud brick with thatch or slate roofs. The majority of Nepalese live in small villages.

Food: Rice is the staple food, except for the Sherpas in the hill region where potato is the staple. A typical meal consists of *bhat* (rice), *daal* (lentil gravy), *tarkkaari* (vegetables), and a bit of *achaar* (pickle or chutney). The national drink is tea with milk and sugar; Sherpas drink tea with salt and butter. Devout Hindus do not eat beef, and Muslims abstain from pork. A variety of dairy products are made from milk from yaks, cows, and water buffaloes.

Sports and Recreation: Most festivals are religious in nature. People dress in their finest clothes and gather at a shrine to offer prayers and gifts to the deity. The New Year festival is celebrated in April or May; the eight-day festival of Indra Jatra is celebrated in August or September; and Dasain is a fifteen-day national festival celebrating Rama's triumph over evil spirits. Music and dance are favorite pastimes. Drums, wind instruments, and devotional songs are part of all religious ceremonies. At harvest time people perform the traditional rice dance.

Social Welfare: Village development programs try to provide basic help to the locals. Older and sick people are taken care by family members. Older parents are the responsibility of their children.

IMPORTANT DATES

563 B.C.—Prince Siddhartha Gautama, founder of Buddhism, is born in Lumbini.

249 B C.—Emperor Asoka visits Lumbini.

57 B.C.—Vikram Samvat calendar begins.

A.D. 79—Shakya Samvat calendar begins.

467—An inscription written in the Changu Narayan Temple identifies the Licchavi king Manadeva as the builder of this temple.

879—Newar Samvat calendar begins.

1670—King Pratap Malla builds the Rani Pokhari pool for his wife.

1744—Prithvi Narayan Shah wages the first attack on Nuwakot in an attempt to win Kathmandu Valley.

1766—Prithvi Narayan Shah gains the first foothold in the Kathmandu Valley.

1768—Prithvi Narayan Shah captures Kathmandu Valley from the Malla kings.

1769—The last of the Malla kings is deposed.

1769–1814—Shah dynasty rules and extends the territory of Nepal.

1814—Bhim Sen Shah's troops battle Indians and British along the Indian border.

1816—Peace treaty is signed between Nepal and Britain at Segauli.

1846—Jang Bahadur Rana, a political leader, seizes control of Nepal's government; he declares that a member of his family will serve as prime minister from then on; Rana rule continues until 1951.

1852—British surveyors establish that Mt. Everest is the highest.

1859—Mt. Everest is officially acknowledged as earth's highest peak.

1895—A German archeologist begins to excavate Lumbini's ruins.

1901—Prime Minister Chandra Shamser Rana builds the Singh Durbar in Kathmandu. With 1,700 rooms, it is one of the largest private residences in Asia.

1921—Sir George Mallory of Britain launches the first expedition to climb Mt. Everest.

1924—Sir George Mallory and his climbing partner, Andrew Irvine, disappear while climbing Mt. Everest.

1926—Slavery is abolished and the custom of sati is outlawed.

1934—An earthquake hits Kathmandu.

1936—Nepal's first jute mill opens at Biratnagar.

1940—Revolutionaries try to oust the Ranas (of the Shah dynasty).

1945—Rana Padma Shamsher becomes prime minister.

1946—The Nepali Congress Party is founded.

1947—The United States establishes diplomatic relations with Nepal.

1948—Attempts are made by Prime Minister Padma Shamsher Rana to introduce free elections; the constitution is suspended.

1950—King Tribhuvan is exiled to India, leaving the Ranas in control of the government; Nepal opens its borders to the outside world.

1951—King Tribhuvan returns to Nepal in triumph; he sets up a constitutional monarchy; Rana power ends.

1953—Edmund Hillary and Tenzing Norgay become the first people to reach the peak of Mt. Everest.

1955—King Tribhuvan dies; Nepal joins the United Nations.

1959—A new constitution in enacted; the first national elections are held; Tribhuvan University is founded.

1960—The constitution is suspended and parliament is dissolved; political parties are banned; Sir Edmund Hillary concludes that the Yeti (snowman) does not exist except in people's imagination, but not everyone agrees.

1962—A new constitution has no provision for political parties and establishes the panchayat form of government; the present national flag of Nepal is officially adopted.

1965—Nawang Gopmbu, an Indian Sherpa, becomes the first to reach Mt. Everest summit twice.

1972—King Mahendra Shah dies and is succeeded by King Birendra; administrative development regions are established.

1973—Nepal's first wildlife preserve, Royal Chitwan National Park, opens.

1974—A fire set by rebels destroys most of the Singh Durbar residence.

1975—Junko Tabei of Japan becomes the first woman to reach the peak of Mt. Everest; King Birendra is crowned.

1976—Sagarmatha National Park is established.

1979—Antigovernment demonstrators demand a change in the political system of the country; King Birendra announces a referendum on the panchayat form of government.

1980—The panchayat system is favored by a slim majority in a referendum; National Assembly members are to be elected by popular vote; Reinhold Messner of Italy becomes the first person to climb Mt. Everest solo.

1981—Elections for the National Assembly are held.

1982—The Press Act tightens censorship of the press.

1984—A 300-bed teaching hospital opens.

1985—The outlawed Nepali Congress Party (NCP) holds a convention.

1986—General elections are held; Nepal begins its first television broadcast; Mahendra Sanskrit University is opened.

1987—Top-level government officials are removed in a anticorruption drive.

1989—The southern Dolpo area is opened to foreigners; Thyangboche Monastery burns.

1990—The Movement for the Restoration of Democracy (MRD), a political party, is formed; the panchayat system is abolished; the ban on political parties is lifted, and political and religious prisoners are freed; democracy is established for the first time.

1991—National elections are held; the NCR comes into power.

1992—Communist and other opposition groups organize strikes and demonstrations; Mustang's capital city of Manthang is opened to foreigners; 28 climbers from 5 expeditions reach the summit of Everest in a single day.

1993—Two top officials of the Communist Party of Nepal (United Marxist-Leninist)-CPN (UML) are killed; a nationwide protest follows.

1994—Prime Minister G. P. Koirala resigns; elections are held; UML forms a government; India agrees to establish a 350-bed Institute of Health Sciences at Dharan in Nepal; Nepal opens the forbidden kingdom of Mustang to foreigners.

1995—More than 60 people die in the monsoon floods; Communist government of Prime Minister Manmohan Adhikary is dissolved, and Sher Bahadur Deuba is named prime minister; new general elections are scheduled.

IMPORTANT PEOPLE

Manmohan Adhikary, leader of the Communist Party of Nepal; prime minister from 1994 to 1995; his government was dissolved in 1995.

Amsuvarman, son-in-law of the Licchavi king Shevadeva; declared himself king in 605; married his daughter Bhrikuti to the king of Tibet to strength his kingdom

Arideva, first king of the Malla dynasty

Emperor Asoka (? – 238 or 232 B.C.), a Hindu emperor of India of the Maurya dynasty; converted to Buddhism about 261 B.C. and made it the state religion; built many Buddhist shrines in Nepal and India

Bhanubhakta, nineteenth-century poet

Carumati, Emperor Asoka's daughter; helped her father in spreading the teachings of Buddha

Birendra Bir Bikram Shah Dev (1945–), present king; crowned in 1975; tenth ruler of the Shah dynasty; democratized the panchayat system; reintroduced multiparty system in Nepal

Prince Siddhartha Gautama (563–483 B.C.), founder of Buddhism; known as the Buddha ("Enlightened One"); meditated and achieved enlightenment at the age of 35 (522 B.C.); taught his doctrine of the "Four Noble Truths"

Sir Edmund P. Hillary (1919–   ), native of New Zealand; mountain climber and Antarctic explorer; first person to climb Mt. Everest with his guide Tenzing Norgay in 1953; knighted by the Queen Elizabeth II of Great Britain for this feat

B.P. (Bisweswar Prasad) Koirala (1915–82), head of the Nepali Congress Party and the first elected prime minister of Nepal (1959 to 1960)

Girija Prasad Koirala, party secretary of NCP; prime minister 1991 to 1994

Jayasthiti Malla, reigned from 1382 to 1359; a Hindu king, he laid the foundation of today's Hindu state; declared himself an incarnation of Lord Vishnu (the tradition is still carried on by Nepal's kings)

Pratap Malla, ruled from 1640 to 1674; a literary king also known as "King of Poets"

Siddhi Narasimba Malla (1618–61), known for construction of hundreds of houses in Patan

Yaksha Malla (?–1482), grandson of Jayasthiti Malla; reigned from 1429 to 1482; divided his kingdom among his daughter and three sons

Maya Devi, Siddhartha Gautama's mother; queen of Lumbini

Tenzing Norgay (1914–86), also called Namgyal Wangdi, the first Sherpa to climb Mt. Everest, with Sir Edmund Hillary in 1953

Jung Bahadur Rana (1817–77), a Rana prime minister

Bala Krishna Sama (1903–?), twentieth–century writer and dramatist

Prithvi Narayan Shah (? –1775), became king of Gorkha in 1742; reigned 1769–75; undertook a military campaign to unify the country; he took the title of king of Nepal and his descendants have served as monarchs ever since

Mahendra Bir Bikram Shah (1920–72), son of Tribhuvan Shah; established the partyless panchayat system of government; reigned from 1955 until 1972; a poet, he did much to promote the revival of arts and literature

King Tribhuvan Shah (? –1955), established the constitutional monarchy in Nepal; reigned from 1911 to 1955

Amar Singh Thapa, military leader of the 19th century; a national hero

Hsuan Tsang, Chinese pilgrim; wrote about craftspeople and artists of Nepal in A.D. 637

Wang Hsuan Tse, Chinese emissary; wrote about Kathmandu's palaces and jewels

Compiled by Chandrika Kaul, Ph.D.

INDEX

Page numbers that appear in boldface type indicate illustrations

About the Author

Ann Heinrichs grew up in Arkansas and lives in Chicago. She is the author of eleven books on American and Asian regions and cultures, as well as numerous newspaper, magazine, and encyclopedia articles. In the advertising and marketing fields, her subjects have ranged from plumbing hardware to Oriental rugs. In private life, Ms. Heinrichs is a classical pianist, a desert traveler, and a student of t'ai chi standard and sword forms.